D0274801

MISS HOPE & MR GREENWOOD

SWEETS
MADE SIMPLE

MISS HOPE & MR GREENWOOD

SWEETS
MADE SIMPLE

BOOKS

Falkirk Council	
DY	
Askews & Holts	
641.853	£16.99

CONTENTS

HELLO PLAYMATES!

*It is I, Miss Hope, top-heavy wearer of unsuitable shoes,
and wife to the husband of my dreams (mainly good ones),
the smart-booted, walrus-whiskered Mr Greenwood.
Together we dish out big sweet-shop hugs and stripy
paper bags rustling with the splendid sugar confections
of your childhood.*

*Growing up in the stottie-chomping north-east of England,
I developed an intrinsic love of sweets. My childhood sweet
shop, Campbell's, was a treasure cave of Aladdinesque treats,
in more colours than a cupboard stuffed with harem pants.
Armed with a big flat copper penny, on Sundays, I looked
forward to skipping off to buy liquorice chews and a packet
of sarsaparilla tablets (weird).*

*In my student days in Newcastle I was fortunate to live round
the corner from the sweet shop of sweet shops, Clough's.
It's still there today – the hub of the community, a meeting
place with as much heart as there are sherbet pips.*

Thus inspired, it was only a matter of time before I dragged Mr G away from his well-paid job to join me in a whirl of confectionery and sugar. We decided (I decided) to open a sweet shop in the delightful toon of London. Our shelves heave under a medley of traditional fare: apple and custards, sherbet lemons and toffee bonbons, but we have also set about inventing sweets with new flavours for a whole new generation of sweet lovers.

In this splendid book you will discover a plethora of my top-notch treats, all simple enough to make in your own kitchen. Easy-peasy, lemon-squeezy.

Now, let's begin.

THE RULES

Before we go any further, you ought to know that I am a bit bossy. I expect you to do exactly as you are told, or you will have to stand in the corner until playtime. Isn't that right, Mr Greenwood? So, here we go, first lesson.

PLEASE DO: PAY ATTENTION. When I say 'use a deep heavy-bottomed pan' (4 litres or 5–6 pints big), which I do quite a lot, you simply must or you will end up with toffee down the front of your apron.

PLEASE DO: REFRAIN FROM EATING HOT TOFFEE. It is really, really hot, it will burn you and you will cry. Don't do it, you crazy person, you.

PLEASE DO: BUY A SUGAR THERMOMETER. I beg you on my knees; it doesn't cost too much and it is the tool for the job.

PLEASE DO: WATCH YOUR POTS BOIL. Don't wander off for a bubble bath or pop into Margery's next door with a pie. Some of the recipes need you to stare at the pan while they cook. If you don't, you're in danger of setting the kitchen alight and it will require a crew of firemen to put it out.

PLEASE DO: MELT CHOCOLATE WITH CARE. Melt it using as little heat as possible, as this will stop it going white when it sets, which looks horrible. Take particular care with white chocolate, which melts in no time at all and can burn very easily. It's best to melt couverture chocolate (see page 11).

PLEASE DO: USE A WOODEN SPOON WHEN COOKING TOFFEE, FUDGE AND NOUGAT. A plastic spatula will melt like the Wicked Witch of the West.

PLEASE DO: LEAVE THE SCOURING PAD UNDER THE SINK. The best way to wash a pan covered in toffee or fudge is to fill it with water and put it back on the heat. As if by magic, the toffee will just bubble off.

PLEASE DO: MAKE SWEETS FOR YOUR NEIGHBOURS AND FRIENDS. They will be green with envy for your blissful domestic lifestyle.

SOME DULL BUT IMPORTANT RULES ABOUT TEMPERATURES

Sugar is a fickle thing, one minute it's all 'Coo-wee, look at me, lovely golden bubbling sugar in a pan', and the next thing you are flapping at the smoke alarm with a tea towel.

If you have ignored my advice and not bought a sugar thermometer (tut-tut and shame on you), you can use the following techniques to make my recipes without one.

SOFT BALL

113–118°C (235–245°F) is used for fudges and fondants.

Drop a little of the syrup into a glass of cold water. Leave it for a couple of minutes then roll it between your fingers; it should form a soft ball.

HARD BALL

118–130°C (245–266°F) is used for marshmallows, caramels and nougats.
Drop a little of the syrup into a glass of cold water. Leave it for a couple of minutes then roll it between your fingers, it should form a firm ball, but it should not be rock hard.

SMALL CRACK

132–143°C (270–290°F) is used for toffees and boiled sweets.

Drop a little of the syrup into a glass of cold water. It should separate into small pieces, though they should be hard, not brittle.

HARD CRACK

149–154°C (300–310°F) is used for really hard toffees.

Drop a little of the syrup into a glass of cold water. It should separate into brittle threads and the mixture should start to turn a golden colour.

HOW AND WHY

TO TEMPER CHOCOLATE

If you heat and cool chocolate without controlling the temperature, the crystallisation of cocoa butter will result in crystals of different sizes (bad crystals) forming, and your chocolate will bloom – that is to say it will appear matte and covered with white patches. It will also crumble unpleasantly rather than snap. In order to avoid this you will need to temper your chocolate.

Tempering controls the crystals so that only consistently small crystals are produced, resulting in much better-quality chocolate. I have, wherever possible, avoided the need to temper chocolate completely by rolling my truffles in sugar, cocoa or nuts, but if the recipe requires it and you want your chocolate to be shiny 'snapable', without a white bloom, then temper you must.

When making moulded chocolates that are filled with ganache or a fruity cream filling, you can use couverture chocolate, such as Callebaut or Valrhona, which has a higher cocoa butter content but which does need to be tempered. This will give the chocolates a lovely appetising shine, a pleasing snap when you bite into it and a smooth, melt-in-the-mouth texture without any graininess. If you use regular chocolate, the chocolate will still need to be tempered using the same method.

For all my recipes that require the chocolate to be tempered, please use 300g (11oz) of chocolate for one tray of chocolates and about 450g (1lb) of chocolate for two trays. These quantities will ensure the temperature of the chocolate is maintained while you coat the moulds. Don't worry if you don't use all the tempered chocolate, as you can scrape it into a container, seal it, store it at room temperature and use it later. Before reusing the chocolate, temper it again if you are using it for chocolate shells, or melt it in a bain marie if you're using it to make truffles.

TEMPERING FOR RICH PEOPLE
The easiest but priciest way of tempering chocolate is to buy a tempering machine. This heats up the chocolate very, very slowly then cools it down equally slowly, leaving the finished chocolate silky smooth.

THE TRICKY METHOD FOR SMARTY PANTS PEOPLE

This is a bit of a faff as you need a slab of marble, a sugar thermometer and a metal scraper, thick palette knife or spatula.

First you need to melt the chocolate very gently in a heatproof bowl set over a pan of simmering water – making sure the chocolate doesn't overheat and the bottom of the bowl doesn't touch the water. Then pour around three-quarters of the melted chocolate onto the marble slab. Work it across the slab until it has reached a temperature of 28°C (82°F) – this is where you need to stick the thermometer into the chocolate all over the slab. Using your scraper/palette knife/spatula, scrape the chocolate back into the bowl with the rest of it. Heat all the chocolate very gently, if necessary, or allow the residual heat to bring it back up to a temperature of 31–32°C (88–90°F) for dark chocolate, 30–31°C (86–88°F) for milk chocolate and 27–28°C (80–82°F) for white chocolate. It's now ready to use. Good luck.

THE MIDDLE GROUND FOR PEOPLE WITH A SOCIAL LIFE

If you're going to be making chocolates a lot, buy a chocolate thermometer. They're not very expensive and they will make it easier to temper chocolate accurately. Chop your chocolate evenly and put about two thirds of it in a heatproof bowl. Heat 5cm (2in) water in a pan and pop the bowl on top of the pan, making sure that the bottom of the bowl is not touching the water. Allow the chocolate to melt slowly. Put the thermometer into the bowl and make sure the temperature doesn't go above 42°C (107°F).

Once it's liquid, turn off the heat, remove the bowl from the pan and wrap a clean tea towel round the base to keep it warm. Add the remaining chopped chocolate, pop the thermometer in and stir the chocolate until it reaches 31–32°C (88–90°F) for dark chocolate, 30–31°C (86–88°F) for milk chocolate and 27–28°C (80–82°F) for white chocolate. This will take a while. Once done, it's ready to use.

THE MICROWAVE METHOD FOR PEOPLE WITH JOBS, CHILDREN, PETS, FRIENDS, OR A TRAIN TO CATCH

Pop the chopped-up chocolate into a microwaveable plastic or glass bowl and melt at 800–1000W, checking it every 15 seconds or so and taking care it doesn't overheat. When the chocolate looks nearly melted but there are still a few bits bobbed on top, take it out of the microwave and stir the chocolate gently until smooth. It should have thickened slightly. It's now ready to use.

STORAGE

Really there is little point telling you how to store your confections as they will be eaten faster than you can say 'fasting diet'. But, just in case you are puritanical, wise or delusional here are some thoughts about storage.

FUDGE can be stored in the fridge for up to two weeks; please allow it to warm to room temperature before you eat it. It will also freeze well for two months.

TOFFEES should be kept in an airtight container and will last for a week or so. It helps to wrap the pieces individually in parchment paper or they will stick together in a flash. English Almond Butter Toffee (see page 32) should be kept and served directly from the fridge.

CHOCOLATE TRUFFLES made with fresh cream should be kept in the fridge and eaten within 3–4 days. If you freeze them they will last for two months. As a general rule, all chocolates that are being stored in the fridge should be kept in an airtight container to avoid tainting them with the odours of other food nearby.

MR GREENWOOD'S BUTTERED BRAZILS should be placed in an airtight container and sent directly to Mr Greenwood.

COCONUT ICE should be stored in an airtight container and will last for about a month.

MALLOWS should be stored in an airtight container lined with baking parchment and will last for about four days. They are, however, best eaten as fresh as possible.

NOUGAT should be stored in a cool, dry place for up to four days. I find putting it in the fridge makes it ooze unpleasantly.

TURKISH DELIGHT should be stored in an airtight container lined with parchment dusted with icing sugar and cornflour; it will last for about one month.

PASTILLES should be kept in the fridge and last a fleeting two days.

The **CHEWY** sweets can be kept in the fridge for up to five days. Toss the jellies through their sugar coating just before serving.

BISCUITS, PALMIERS AND FLORENTINES should be stored in an airtight container and will keep for 2–3 days.

MISS HOPE should be stored on her sofa with a gin and tonic and a copy of *Sweet Spot Weekly*, her décolletage should be lightly dusted in icing sugar and perfumed with violet syrup. She should last another 30 years or so.

CHAPTER
№ 1

FUDGE,
CARAMEL
and TOFFEE

BLACK FOREST FUDGE

the creamiest chocolatey fudge

MAKES

49

SQUARES MADE IN HEAVEN

Black Forest Dynasty
Helga and Johannes also produced three sons: Ritter, Oetker (who became a famous doctor) and Vorsprung Durch Technik.

Once upon a time there was a master baker called Johannes. Johannes lived in the Black Forest where he gathered berries to make his famous Black Forest Gateau. One day he fell in love with a comely dairy maid called Helga. Their marriage produced this recipe for the creamiest chocolatey fudge, studded with rich sticky cherries.

Takes around 30 minutes to make; plus cooling and overnight chilling.

40g (1½oz) unsalted butter, plus extra to grease
75g (3oz) dark glacé cherries
500g (1lb 2oz) golden caster sugar
275ml (10fl oz) double cream
75g (3oz) dark chocolate, grated
50g (2oz) white chocolate, grated

❦ Generously butter (less than a turkey buttering, more than a slimmer's sandwich) a 17cm (6¾in) square tin and line it with baking parchment. Cut 50g (2oz) of the sticky cherries in half, then quarter the remaining fruits.

❦ Put the sugar, cream and butter in a large, heavy-bottomed pan (I use a deep 24cm (9½ in) diameter pan) with 3 tablespoons of water. Please heat gently for 5–10 minutes to dissolve the sugar. Thank you.

❦ Pop a sugar thermometer in the pan and bring the liquid up to the boil. Boil until the thermometer reaches 113°C (235°F).

❦ Take the pan off the heat and pour around a third of the mixture into a metal bowl. Add the dark chocolate to the remaining mixture in the pan and the white chocolate to the metal bowl. Stir each with separate spoons until they begin to thicken.

❦ Now for the fun bit. Pour the dark chocolate into the square tin. Sprinkle over the quartered cherries. Spoon over the white chocolate, then drag a skewer through the mixture to create swirls all over.

❦ Dot the halved cherries over the top, allow to cool, then chill overnight until set. Remove from the tin and cut into squares.

PEANUT BUTTER FUDGE

the ultimate face-mask fudge

Handy Hint
Please pop the finished fudge into a parcel and post it to: Miss Hope, 42 Peanut House, Peanut Head, Peanutsville.

MAKES

50

SQUARES OF SALTY JOY

I love peanut butter; I can't get enough of it. It is exceptional in a bacon sandwich or as a face mask, and it is beyond my wildest nut fantasies when added to this creamy fudge. I am informed that my American chums eat 3 pounds of peanut butter per person every year; apparently that's enough to cover the floor of the Grand Canyon. Now that would make your wellies sticky.

Takes 30 minutes to make; a couple of hours to set.

500g (1lb 2oz) caster sugar
250ml (8fl oz) evaporated milk
2 tbsp double cream
100g (4oz) unsalted butter
2 large rounded tbsp crunchy peanut butter

❀ Line a 20cm (8in) square baking tin, 4cm (1½in) deep, with baking parchment.

❀ Place the sugar, evaporated milk, double cream and butter into a large deep heavy-bottomed pan over a gentle heat. Stir the mixture with a wooden spoon until the sugar has dissolved – this takes about 5 minutes.

❀ Turn up the heat to medium, place your sugar thermometer in the pan and bring the mixture to the boil – it will double in size, so put the cat in a safe place.

❀ Bring the mixture up to 100°C (215°F), stirring occasionally, then lower the heat to a gentle boil. Boil for a further 10 minutes, stirring more frequently now as it does have a tendency to catch and caramelise on the bottom. Take care when the thermometer reaches 118°C (244°F), as at this point the mixture burns easily. Remove from the heat.

❀ Using an electric hand whisk or food processor, or indeed a wooden spoon, beat the mixture for 5 minutes and then add the peanut butter. Beat for a further 5–10 minutes or until the mixture loses its shine, thickens up and starts to appear grainy. Pour into the prepared tin.

❀ Set aside to cool. After about 1 hour, score the surface into rough squares with a knife. Once cold and firm, break into squares.

HONEY & ALMOND WHITE CHOCOLATE FUDGE

suitable for bears of all ages

MAKES

50

HONEYED PIECES – 40 TO
SERVE AND 10 TO EAT

Last night I discovered two bears on my sofa surrounded by the remnants of my Honey & Almond White Chocolate Fudge. Honestly, bears take such liberties; using my shampoo, leaving their wet towels on the floor, playing loud music, girls coming and going at all hours. They treat this place like a hotel.

Takes a good 40 minutes of your time, plus cooling and chilling.

25g (1oz) unsalted butter, plus extra to grease
400g (14oz) caster sugar
300ml (½ pint) double cream
2 tsp clear honey
25g (1oz) white chocolate, roughly chopped
50g (2oz) whole almonds, toasted and roughly chopped
50g (2oz) ready-to-eat dried apricots, roughly chopped

● Generously butter a 17cm (6¾in) square baking tin and line with baking parchment. Plonk the butter, sugar, cream and honey in a large heavy-bottomed pan (I use a deep 24cm (9½in) diameter pan). Heat gently and stir the mixture together. You must make sure all the sugar has dissolved, so test it by dipping the back of a teaspoon into the mixture and running your finger or tongue down it. Keep heating and stirring on a gentle heat if any grains remain.

● As soon as all the sugar has dissolved, turn up the heat to medium until you get a rolling boil. Continue to stir the mixture for about 15 minutes. It will metamorphose from looking a bit like a white sauce to the beautiful colour of thick-set honey.

● Take the pan off the heat. If you are astute you will notice the mixture still bubbling up now; it looks delicious but don't, even if you are wilful, be tempted to stick any part of your anatomy in it. Stir in the chocolate, almonds and apricots. Beat well for 5–10 minutes until the mixture loses its shine and gloss and becomes thick and pasty.

● Spoon into the prepared tin and smooth over. Leave to cool, then chill to set. Remove the fudge from the tin, cut into squares and dance a dance with waggly arms, like a spider-monkey-crab-beast.

FUDGE FOR CHEATS

with a bit of cooking

MAKES

49

JOLLY PIECES

This fudge is absolutely perfect if you are just not in the mood for thermometers and all that gubbins. It's also a cracking recipe if you have keen little chefs. There is some heating involved but with a little supervision they will find the stirring bit fun. Feel free to add your own favourite ingredients. Here I've used sugar-coated chocolates, because I like them, but you could use jelly buttons, chocolate buttons or sprinkles.

Takes around 15 minutes to make, plus chilling.

60g (2½oz) unsalted butter, chopped, plus extra to grease
125g (4½oz) milk chocolate, chopped
125g (4½oz) dark chocolate, chopped
200g condensed milk (NOT evaporated milk)
1 tsp vanilla extract
sugar-coated chocolates or other sweets of your choice

* Generously butter a 17cm (6¾in) square tin and line with baking parchment.
* Heat 5cm (2in) water in a pan. Pop a heatproof bowl on top of the pan, making sure the bottom of the bowl is not touching the water. Add the two types of chocolate, the butter, condensed milk and vanilla extract to the bowl.
* Reduce the heat to the lowest setting and allow the chocolate and butter to melt.
* Take the pan off the heat and have fun stirring all the ingredients together. Please be careful, you nana, the bowl is hot.
* Pour into the prepared tin and scatter over your chosen sugar-coated chocolates or sweets, pushing them gallantly into the fudge so that they stick. Cool, then chill overnight.
* Remove from the fridge, cut into squares and get stuck in.

GINGERBREAD LATTE FUDGE

the fudge equivalent of wincyette pyjamas

MAKES
49
SPLENDID SQUARES

Every winter I look forward to the comfort and spice of a gingerbread latte so what better than to take the whole exquisite experience and fold some old school sticky ginger cake, cream and coffee into a smooth, yielding fudge with a frothy latte topping? Every winter I also look forward to hot water bottles, winceyette nighties and bed socks. Poor Mr Greenwood.

Takes about 40 minutes to make, plus chilling.

50g (2oz) salted butter, plus extra for greasing
75g (2½oz) sticky ginger cake, thinly sliced
500g (1lb 2oz) caster sugar
150ml (5fl oz) double cream
135ml (4½fl oz) full-fat milk
1 tsp ground ginger
2 tsp ground espresso coffee

🍪 Boldly butter a 17cm (6¾in) square tin and line with baking parchment. Preheat your grill to medium.

🍪 Now lay the ginger cake slices on a baking sheet. Grill until toasted on both sides. Allow to cool and then chop it up roughly. Taste to make sure it's lovely.

🍪 Now put the sugar, cream, milk, butter and 3 tablespoons of water in a large deep pan (I use a 24cm (9½in) diameter pan) and heat gently over a very low heat for about 15 minutes, until the sugar has dissolved.

🍪 Wedge a sugar thermometer into the pan and turn the heat up a notch until the mixture starts to bubble. Hold it at this point, adjusting the heat accordingly, and cook until the mixture reaches 116°C (240°F). If you don't have a thermometer, cook at this steady pace for about 15 minutes. Give the mixture a stir every now and then.

🍪 As soon as the temperature has been reached, pour about a quarter of the ooze into a metal bowl and set aside. Add the ginger and coffee to the pan and beat it with vigour for a minute. Stir in the chopped cake, which dissolves into the mixture, and continue to beat well for 5–8 minutes until the mixture has cooled a little and starts to thicken round the edge. It'll be coming away from the edges of the pan.

🍪 Pour into the prepared tin. Give the plain fudge mixture a quick beat and spoon dollops over the top. Use a skewer to marble the layers – it should look fluffy like a latte. Allow to cool then chill for a couple of hours. Cut into squares and eat.

PULLED BUTTER TOFFEE

the work-out toffee

Handy Hint
A rubber glove will give you the power you need to twist off any stubborn screwtop lid.

MAKES

30

GOOD TWISTS

This recipe is ideal if you are bothered by bingo arms, have a blacksmith as a neighbour or throw the shot-put as a hobby. You will need the strength of an ox, sir, and rubber gloves to make this very traditional butter toffee. It is enormous fun to make – with dramatic huffing and puffing, pulling and twisting. Next year I may bring out the accompanying fitness DVD.

Takes 30 minutes to make; a couple of hours to cool.

groundnut oil, for greasing
225g (8oz) granulated sugar
75ml (3fl oz) water
50g (2oz) unsalted butter
¼ tsp cream of tartar

You will also need a pair of rubber gloves oiled with groundnut oil. (Yes, this is going to be fun all the way!)

❦ Lightly oil a 39 × 35cm (15¼ × 13¾in) baking sheet.

❦ Put the sugar, water, butter and cream of tartar into a small heavy-bottomed pan (I use one with a 13cm/5in base). Heat the mixture on a moderate heat, stirring all the time until the sugar has dissolved. Place a sugar thermometer in the pan, bring the mixture to the boil and bubble until your sugar thermometer reaches 137°C (280°F).

❦ Quick as sticks, pour the mixture onto the prepared baking sheet in an oozy puddle. Be careful it is hotter than a leopard's tail in a microwave.

❦ Once it is cool enough to handle (after about 10–15 minutes), don your groundnut-oiled rubber gloves.

❦ Lift the puddle off the parchment and roughly push it together to make a rough ball. Now pull each side apart to make two long strings. Join the ends together and twist. Take each end again and stretch the toffee out like a long sausage, then take the ends and fold them into the middle. Take hold of the two 'new' ends and pull them out like a sausage again, fold them into the centre and keep repeating. Keep doing this until your rubber gloves are exhausted (about 10 or 15 times). The toffee will turn into spaghetti-type strands. It doesn't matter if the toffee breaks, just squeeze it back together again. Now twist the strands together like a corkscrew to form tight barley twists. Chop into 2.5cm (1in) long sticks using a sharp knife.

❦ Wrap in individual parchment twists or pretty cellophane. The toffee will last longer than your granny so long as it is wrapped and kept dry.

SALT LIQUORICE CARAMELS

caramels for salt heads

MAKES
64
CARAMELS

Liquorice is part-sweet, part-medicine. It is good for everything: the heart, stomach, colds, ulcers and spots. Roman soldiers kept some in their toga pockets and Napoleon sucked it to cure his bad breath.

Take 30 minutes-ish to make; cool and set overnight.

groundnut oil, for greasing
125g (4½oz) unsalted butter
225g (8oz) granulated sugar
200g (7oz) condensed milk
175ml (6oz) golden syrup
a couple of good pinches
   of rock salt
10g raw liquorice powder
¼ tsp black food colouring
   paste

🟤 Grease a 20cm (8in) square baking tin, 4cm (1½in) deep, with groundnut oil, then line with baking parchment and grease again.

🟤 Place the butter in a deep heavy-bottomed pan with the sugar, condensed milk and golden syrup. Heat over the lowest heat. Once the syrup has melted, stir constantly with a wooden spoon to dissolve the sugar.

🟤 Put a sugar thermometer in the pan and increase the heat slightly to bring the mixture to a gentle boil. Cook, stirring all the time until the temperature reaches 118°C (245°F). Don't worry if brown bits rise up and float around in the mixture, it's just caramelising.

🟤 Take the pan off the heat and use a wooden spoon to stir in a good pinch of rock salt, the liquorice powder and black food colouring. Beat furiously until the black paste ribbons through the mixture then colours it completely. The mixture should be black: black as night, black as a black sheep from the valley.

🟤 Pour the caramel into the prepared tin and scatter with rock salt. Leave to cool for 1 hour then chill. Leave overnight before removing from the fridge and cutting into squares. Wrap each square in a jolly twist of parchment paper.

PENUCHE

Hawaiian digits of fudge

MAKES

34

FINGERS OF FUDGE

The Origins of Penuche

The origins of penuche are somewhat confusing; some say it comes from New England, some say Hawaii. The word 'panocha' comes from the Spanish word for raw sugar.

Penuche (pronounced puh-noo-chee) is part fudge, part candy. What distinguishes it from 'normal' fudge is the caramelised brown sugar that gives the penuche its beautiful colour; in fact it is not unlike the slim digit of fudge of our childhoods. So, if you fancy a change from the paler, British style of fudge, this is for you – made with soft light brown sugar, dark chocolate and vanilla. If you are looking for a more radical change I have no objection, so long as you don't stretch my shoes.

Takes about 1 hour 15 minutes to make, including cooling.

40g (1½oz) unsalted butter, chopped, plus extra to grease
500g (1lb 2oz) soft light brown sugar
225ml (8fl oz) full-fat milk
a good pinch of salt
1 tsp vanilla extract
50g (2oz) dark chocolate

● Generously butter a 17cm (6¾in) square tin and line with baking parchment.

● Put the sugar, milk and salt in a large, heavy-bottomed pan (I use a deep 24cm (9½in) diameter pan). Heat gently for around 3–5 minutes to dissolve the sugar. Pop a sugar thermometer into the pan, bring the mixture up to the boil and continue to cook, stirring all the time, until the temperature reaches 113°C (235°F).

● Take the pan off the heat and dot over the chopped butter. Set aside for 30–45 minutes for the butter to melt and the mixture to cool. It's cool enough to beat together when you can comfortably hold your hand on the bottom of the pan.

● When the mixture has cooled, add the vanilla extract and stir everything together. You'll need to work the butter in; keep at it, as it will eventually blend into the mixture. Continue to beat just until the mixture loses its gloss. Just think of your mother-in-law and how she watches you over the top of her glasses – not quite good enough, are you?

● Quickly pour the fudge into the prepared tin and set aside until firm.

● Heat 5cm (2in) water in a pan. Pop a heatproof bowl on top of the pan, making sure the bottom of the bowl is not touching the water. Place the chocolate in the bowl and allow it to melt slowly. Drizzle it lovingly over the fudge then put it aside to set.

● Take the fudge out of the tin, plonk it on a board, then cut it in half and cut across into squares.

ENGLISH ALMOND BUTTER TOFFEE

the George Clooney of toffees

MAKES

25

LUMPS OF ALMOND HEAVEN

Almond Butter Toffee is, without question, the George Clooney of toffees. If I were the last woman on earth and I had to choose between Clooney and his big packet of English Almond Butter Toffee (and the existence of mankind depended on it), I'd definitely choose the packet.

Takes 30 minutes to make; about 6 hours in total to cool and set.

groundnut oil, for greasing
400g (14oz) flaked almonds
450g (15oz) unsalted butter
500g (1lb 2oz) granulated sugar
1 tsp vanilla extract
200g (7oz) milk chocolate,
   broken into small pieces

● Preheat the oven to 180°C/350°F/Gas 4. Grease a 42 × 27cm (16½ × 10¾in) baking tin, 4cm (1½in) deep, with groundnut oil.

● Place the almonds on a clean baking sheet and roast in the oven for 15 minutes, turning them over and around after 2 minutes and taking care not to singe the edges. Remove from the oven once golden and set aside to cool.

● Place the butter in a deep, heavy-bottomed pan and melt it gently. Add the sugar and stir until it has dissolved. Place a sugar thermometer in the pan, bring the mixture to the boil and bubble on a medium heat until the thermometer reaches 120°C (250°F). This takes about 5 minutes.

● Add three-quarters of the toasted almonds and the vanilla extract to the sugar and butter mixture and give it a couple of brisk stirs with a wooden spoon. The mixture will bubble up a fair bit, so I have warned you. Pour off any excess oil.

● Bring the mixture back to a rolling boil and, on a moderate heat, bubble slowly and steadily for around 15 minutes until the thermometer reaches 150°C (310°F). Take care, it will stay forever at 135°C (275°F) and then whoosh up to 148°C (300°F). (This will take about 5 minutes.)

As soon as the temperature nudges 150°C (310°F), whip the pan off the heat and pour the golden mixture into the prepared baking tin. Don't worry if it looks a little oily, just pour off the oil and discard it. Leave to cool for 1 hour.

Place the small pieces of chocolate evenly over the top of the still-warm toffee and leave to melt. Spread out the chocolate with a palette knife.

Grind the remaining almonds in a coffee grinder until roughly crumbed and scatter the crumbs over the melted chocolate, pressing down to make them stick. Leave to cool.

To remove the toffee from the tin, take a flat screwdriver or toffee hammer, stick it into the toffee and give it a good bash. Break the toffee into chunks and store in the fridge.

Handy Hint
For some reason this toffee tastes best when served directly from the fridge.

CHOCOLATE ORANGE CARAMELS

more tasteful than my Granny's carpet

MAKES
25
CARAMEL SQUARES

My sweet, zesty Chocolate Orange Caramels are dee-licious and considerably more tasteful than my granny's 1970s carpet.

Take 30 minutes
to make; cool and
set overnight.

groundnut oil, for greasing
40g (1½oz) butter
225g (8oz) granulated sugar
150ml (¼ pint) golden syrup
200g (7oz) condensed milk
50g (2oz) orange chocolate bar,
   broken into small pieces
finely grated zest
   of 1 orange

❊ Grease a 20cm (8in) square baking tin, 4cm (1½in) deep, with groundnut oil.

❊ Place the butter in a large, deep heavy-bottomed pan and gently and slowly heat it until it melts. Add the sugar, golden syrup and condensed milk and continue to heat over a moderate heat, stirring constantly with a wooden spoon, until the sugar has dissolved.

❊ Put your trusty sugar thermometer in the pan, bring the mixture to the boil and bubble until the thermometer reaches 110°C (230°F) – this takes 10–15 minutes. It should be golden in colour, like a retriever. Add the broken chocolate and stir briefly.

❊ Bubble again, this time bringing the mixture up to 123°C (255°F); this will take 5 minutes. The mixture should be a darkish caramel colour, like a spray tan. Take the pan off the heat and stir in the grated orange zest.

❊ Pour the caramel into the greased tin and leave to cool for 1 hour, then mark out squares in the surface with a knife. Leave to cool overnight before cutting into squares. Wrap each square in a twist of parchment paper.

Handy Hint
These caramels taste even better when left to mature for a few days. Age before beauty, and all that.

CINDER TOFFEE

explodo volcanic crunchiness

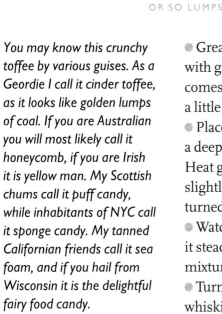

MAKES

20

OR SO LUMPS

Handy Hint
To make honeycomb ice cream, add crumbles of Cinder Toffee to a top-notch vanilla ice cream.

You may know this crunchy toffee by various guises. As a Geordie I call it cinder toffee, as it looks like golden lumps of coal. If you are Australian you will most likely call it honeycomb, if you are Irish it is yellow man. My Scottish chums call it puff candy, while inhabitants of NYC call it sponge candy. My tanned Californian friends call it sea foam, and if you hail from Wisconsin it is the delightful fairy food candy.

Whatever you call it, this toffee is by far the most dramatic to make; it volcanically bubbles to the top of your pan while being heated.

Takes 30 minutes to make;
2 hours to cool and set.

groundnut oil, for greasing
75g (3oz) granulated sugar
25g (1oz) golden syrup
100g (4oz) liquid glucose
1 tbsp water
15g (½oz) bicarbonate of soda

❧ Grease a 17cm (6¾in) square baking tin (4cm/1½in deep) with groundnut oil and line with baking parchment so that it comes about 2.5cm (1in) up the sides, then grease again with a little oil.

❧ Place the sugar, golden syrup, liquid glucose and water, into a deep, heavy-bottomed pan. (When I say deep, I mean deep!) Heat gently to dissolve the sugar, then increase the heat very slightly, stirring every now and then, until the mixture has turned into a syrup.

❧ Watch the pan very carefully from this point on, boiling it steadily at that lowish heat for a good 5 minutes, until the mixture turns amber. It should be the colour of marmalade.

❧ Turn the heat off and stir in the bicarbonate of soda, whisking it all together with a balloon whisk. It will bubble up like a foaming sea right to the top of the pan; you will squeal with excitement and probably wish you had used a bigger pan. Don't say I didn't warn you . . .

❧ Immediately pour the toffee into the prepared tin and leave to cool. When cold, prise the toffee out of the tin using a flat knife and break it up into chunks. If it is difficult to release from the tin, whack it with a hammer; I usually find this works for practically everything in life.

SEASHELL CARAMELS

oh I do like a sea salt caramel

MAKES
20
SEASHELL CHOCOLATES

Mr G and I often take a trip to the South Coast with a little gas stove and a packet of sausages. I was sitting watching the sea as it furled its white fingers around my flip-flops when the idea of popping oozing salted caramel inside a two-chocolate seashell came to me.

'I am quite brilliant,' says I, zipping up my cagoule.

'Harumph,' mumbles Mr G.

Take 25 minutes to make, plus chilling and cooling time.

dark chocolate, for tempering
55ml (2fl oz) double cream
½ level tbsp dark
  muscovado sugar
15g (½oz) caster sugar
a good pinch of sea salt crystals
white chocolate, for tempering

You will also need chocolate moulds with 20 assorted seashells (please see page 186 for stockists)

❀ First up please temper the dark chocolate (see page 11) and use a brush or a teaspoon to coat and line the seashell moulds. Do this quickly or suffer the consequences. Use a sharp knife or chocolate scraper tongue to tidy up any messy bits around the chocolate shells. Scrape any dark chocolate that you haven't used into a bowl and save it to use again, unlikely I know. Slide the moulds into the fridge to set for around 20 minutes .

❀ To make the salted caramel, put the cream and dark muscovado sugar into a small, high-sided heatproof bowl and rest it in a heatproof bowl of boiling water to warm gently.

❀ Pour the caster sugar into a small heavy-bottomed pan and lodge on a low to medium heat to dissolve the sugar, stirring it now and then until it is dark and golden.

❀ Whip the pan off the heat and slop in the warmed cream and muscovado – step away from the pan as it will bubble up. Once the initial bubbling subsides, get a wooden spoon in there and stir furiously, faster, faster, to make a lovely caramel. Cool a wee bit, then stir in the salt.

❀ When the caramel is cool, whip the chocolate moulds out of the fridge and divide the caramel amongst the chocolate shells.

❀ Temper the white chocolate, as before. Spoon the chocolate over the caramel to cover. Chill again for 15 minutes – try a warm bath or a bit of telly. When hard, gently upturn the mould onto a board with a persuasive thumbing and release the chocolates.

❀ Store in an airtight container in the fridge for up to 5 days.

CHIPOTLE, ALMOND & SEA SALT TOFFEE

the inferno

Chipotle (pronounced chi-pot-lay) is a dried smoked chilli, which originates in Mexico. Here I've combined it with a thick, toffee crunch, have added a splash of sea salt and finished it with a snowfall of sweet coconut. Chipotle was first discovered by the infamous chilli eater Samuel Sparks, 'The Inferno', who toured American fairgrounds in his custom-built Firemobile demonstrating his super-hot chilli-imbibing skills.

Takes 40 minutes to make, plus setting and chilling.

225g (8oz) unsalted butter, plus extra for greasing
125g (4½oz) flaked almonds
25g (1oz) desiccated coconut
250g (9oz) granulated sugar
2 tsp chipotle sauce
75g (3oz) dark chocolate
30g (1oz) coconut flakes

❋ Grease and line a 17cm (6¾in) square tin with baking parchment.

❋ Now toast the flaked almonds in a pan over a medium heat, tossing with abandon every now and then until beautifully golden. Take the pan off the heat and stir in the desiccated coconut – the heat of the pan will subtly toast the coconut, too. Yummilicious.

❋ Whack the butter and sugar in a heavy-bottomed pan and allow them to melt very slowly over the lowest heat – this will take 15–20 minutes. Stir the mixture to help it on its way until you have an angelic, creamy white mixture.

❋ Stick a sugar thermometer into the pan and cook until the mixture reaches 120°C (250°F).

❋ Take the pan off the heat and tip in the nut mixture. Stir furiously to mix it all together and pour off any oil that comes out. Put the pan back over a medium heat and replace the thermometer. Stir well for about 5 minutes, watching the temperature like a hawk until it reaches 150°C (300°F).

❋ Spoon the toffee into the tin and leave for 30 minutes to cool.

❋ Melt the chocolate in a heatproof bowl resting over a pan of simmering water, making sure the base of the bowl doesn't touch the water. Spoon over the toffee, teasing it round to the edges with a knife.

❋ Toast the coconut flakes in a dry frying pan until just golden. Whizz in a mini blender or attack with a knife until roughly chopped and sprinkle over the chocolate. Allow to set then chill.

CHAPTER Nº2
CHOCOLATEY

PEPPERMINT CRACKERS

a charming alternative to toothpaste

MAKES
15–20
SOOTHING SQUARES

Handy Hint
Stir the peppermint cracknel with a wooden spoon while heating to dissolve the sugar, but use the back of a metal spoon to check for any remaining sugar crystals.

During the Middle Ages the smiley folk of Great Britain used crushed peppermint to whiten their teeth; it is also known to scare off mice. This recipe combines a soothing mint cracknel running through a sliver of dark chocolate. I don't believe it will scare off mice, but I urge you to give it a go as toothpaste.

Take 30 minutes to make; cool and set overnight.

125g (4½ oz) unsalted butter, plus extra for greasing
250g (9oz) dark chocolate, broken into small bits
2 tbsp golden syrup
2 tbsp cocoa powder

For the peppermint cracknel
100g (4oz) granulated sugar
100ml (4fl oz) water
5 drops of peppermint oil

🍫 Grease a 39 × 35cm (15¼ × 13¾in) baking sheet with butter.

🍫 First, make the peppermint cracknel. Place the sugar and water into a heavy-bottomed pan over a low heat. Stir continuously with a wooden spoon until the sugar has dissolved – this takes about 3 minutes (see Handy Hint, above). Add the peppermint oil and stir.

🍫 Bring the mixture to a boil and, without stirring, boil gently for around 10 minutes until the syrup is a golden brown. Tip the mixture out onto the greased baking sheet and leave to cool.

🍫 Place the chocolate, butter, golden syrup and cocoa into a heatproof bowl and place over a pan of simmering water, taking care that the base of the bowl does not touch the water. Melt the chocolate slowly. Stir everything together, then remove from the heat.

🍫 Using a rolling pin, crush the cooled peppermint cracknel into small shards. Add the shards to the chocolate mixture and mix well.

🍫 Line a 20cm (8in) square baking tin with baking parchment. Pour the mixture into the tin and cool. Once cold, turn the chocolate slab out onto a board, remove the parchment and cut into cracker-sized squares.

CHERRY CHAPEL HAT PEGS

a romantic journey of cherryness

MAKES

20

HAT PEGS

So, you old romantic you, here are my amazing ganache-rich, liqueur-soaked cherry chapel hat pegs for your edification. Grown men will throw their caps in the air, ladies swoon in the street, and grandad will reminisce about Betty Bright, his first love.

Take 1 week to soak the cherries; 30 minutes to make; then cool and set overnight.

1 jar of maraschino cherries
kirsch or cherry brandy (you
    will use about a ¼ bottle)
450g (1lb) dark chocolate,
    broken into small bits
200ml (7fl oz) double cream
25g (1oz) unsalted butter
1 tsp groundnut oil

20 sweet cases (optional)

Get ahead: empty the liquid out of the cherry jar and fill it right up to the top with kirsch or cherry brandy instead. Put the lid back on and leave it for a week to hibernate. After a week, drain the cherries, reserving the liquid.

Line a 39 × 35cm (15¼ × 13¾in) baking sheet with baking parchment.

Put 200g (7oz) of the broken chocolate into a bowl.

Pop the cream and butter into a saucepan and heat until simmering, without letting it boil. Be careful it does not burn or catch on the bottom of the pan.

Take the pan off the heat, pour it over the chocolate and give it a brisk stir. Set aside, but check it to make sure that all the chocolate has melted. Give it a stir to help it along if need be. Add 2 tablespoons of the reserved kirsch and stir.

Cool the mixture for an hour or so and then spoon dollops the size of a pound/euro/quarter coin onto the baking sheet. Once you have 20 dollops, go back and pop another dollop on top of the original dollop – try to keep the dollops quite tall.

Place a cherry on top of each dollop, pressing it down slightly. Chill for around 30 minutes to allow the ganache to set.

Temper the remaining chocolate following the method on page 11.

Take each cherry dollop and squeeze the ganache to shape it into a round. Using two forks, dip into the melted dark chocolate to coat. Place the dollop onto the baking parchment. Continue until all the dollops are coated then leave to cool and set.

Handy Hint
Gild the lily.

VERY BAD S'MORES

a shocking, dribbly mess

MAKES

4

S'MORES

First recorded in the Girl Scout Handbook of 1927, s'mores (give me 'some more') are an American campfire treat, the delights of which have been tragically overlooked in Blighty. In my 'no-bonfire-required' version, gooey mallows, runny chocolate and digestive biscuits are all squished together in a shocking, oozy, dribbly mess. (Have plenty of wet wipes and perhaps a spare clean T-shirt to hand!)

Take 5 minutes to make.

4 squares of dark or
   milk chocolate
8 digestive biscuits
8 pink and white
   marshmallows
dulce de leche toffee sauce

❀ Preheat the grill to medium. On a baking sheet, place 1 square of chocolate onto 4 of the digestive biscuits. Top each with 2 mallows and drizzle over a dollop of toffee sauce.

❀ Place the biscuits under the grill until brown and bubbling. Remove from the heat.

❀ Squidge the remaining 4 digestive biscuits on top.

VARIATIONS

❀ Swap the toffee sauce for peanut butter.

❀ Add chocolate ice cream after you have grilled the mallows.

❀ Use pieces of orange chocolate instead of milk chocolate.

❀ Use ginger snap biscuits instead of digestive biscuits.

COFFEE CREAMS

my Uncle John's favourite nibble

MAKES

18

CREAMS

My Coffee Creams are made with a secret ingredient – marshmallows – for extra unctuousness, then topped off with a pert, chocolate-coated coffee bean. Smooth and perky, they are my Uncle John's favourite treat.

Take 30 minutes to make; plus overnight drying then setting.

50g (2oz) white marshmallows
125g (4½oz) icing sugar, plus extra for dusting (optional)
2 tsp coffee essence or 2 tsp cooled strong coffee
dark chocolate, for tempering
18 chocolate-covered coffee beans

● Fluff the marshmallows in a bowl and add ½ tablespoon of water. Microwave on High for 1 minute, if you are modern, or melt carefully in a pan on the hob. Stir to dissolve any little blobs of drowning marshmallows, bashing them with a wooden spoon if they resist death. Remove from the heat.

● Add the icing sugar and coffee essence and mix together. You may wish to wear rubber gloves. Tip out onto a clean board and knead well to mix in the icing sugar – you may need an extra fairy sprinkling of icing sugar to stop it sticking.

● Pick off walnut-sized knobs of the mixture and shape them into balls. Rub them together to make a chipolata shape and press one side down on the board so that it has a flat bottom. Leave them to dry on baking parchment for about 6 hours.

● Temper the chocolate (see page 11). Put a wire cooling rack over a board or baking sheet. Use a chocolate dipping fork or table fork to plunge the coffee sweets into the chocolate. Lift out, let the excess chocolate dribble back into the bowl and set them on the rack. When you've covered all the coffee sweets, dip each coffee bean into the chocolate and set one on top of each sweet. Leave to set.

ROSE AND VIOLET CREAMS

a meander through my walled garden

MAKES
40
'NO-COOK' EASY-PEASY FONDANT ROSE
CREAMS AND VIOLET CREAMS

*The sun is shining, briefly.
Take my arm and let us stroll
at leisure through my walled
garden, plucking the occasional
pink cabbage rose and letting
our skirts skim the delicate
petals of the shrinking violets.
All too soon it will be time to
put the bins out, feed the cat
and microwave an ocean pie.*

Take 40 minutes to make;
cool and set overnight.

Rose Creams
pink food colouring
2 tbsp rose syrup
300–325g (11–11½oz)
   fondant icing sugar
300–400g (11–14oz) milk
   chocolate, broken into
   small bits
20 crystallised rose petals,
   to decorate

20 sweet cases (optional)

LET'S START WITH THE ROSE CREAMS

❀ Place 1 drop (yes, only 1 drop) of pink food colouring and the rose syrup into a bowl and mix well.

❀ Sift the icing sugar over the syrup mixture and stir to combine. This is a little like making pizza dough, so tip the mixture out onto a worksurface lightly dusted with icing sugar and knead the fondant with your hands until it all comes together in a firm ball. Place the fondant in the fridge for about 30 minutes to firm up.

❀ Using your hands, roll teaspoon-sized lumps of mixture into balls then flatten them slightly and place on a large plate. Continue until you have a plate full of flattened discs.

❀ Heat 5cm (2in) water in a pan until simmering. Pop a heatproof bowl on top of the pan, making sure that the bottom of the bowl is not touching the water. Place the milk chocolate and the groundnut oil in the bowl and warm until melted. Remove from the heat and cool for 10 minutes.

❀ Line a 39 × 35cm (15¼ × 13¾in) baking sheet with baking parchment. Carefully take a fondant disc, one at a time, and, using two forks, dip it in the melted chocolate until coated all over. Be quick about it, as you don't want to melt the fondant. Place the coated fondant onto the baking parchment.

➦

Violet Creams . . .
purple food colouring
2 tbsp violet syrup
300–325g (11–11½oz)
    fondant icing sugar
300–400g (11–14oz) dark
    chocolate, broken into
    small bits
20 crystallised violet petals,
    to decorate

20 sweet cases (optional)

Continue until all the discs are coated. Top each chocolate with a crystallised rose petal and leave to cool and set in a cool place. Place in sweet cases to serve, if you like.

NOW FOR VIOLET CREAMS . . .

● Place the purple food colouring and the violet syrup into a bowl and mix well.

● Sift the icing sugar over the syrup mixture and stir to combine. This is a little like making pizza dough, so tip the mixture out onto a worksurface lightly dusted with icing sugar and knead the fondant with your hands until it all comes together in a firm ball. Place the fondant in the fridge to firm up for about 30 minutes.

● Take the fondant out of the fridge and, using your hands, roll teaspoon-sized lumps of mixture into balls then flatten them slightly and place on a large plate. Continue until you have a plate full of flattened discs.

● Heat 5cm (2in) water in a pan until simmering. Pop a heatproof bowl on top of the pan, making sure that the bottom of the bowl is not touching the water. Place the dark chocolate in the bowl and warm until melted. Remove from the heat and cool for 10 minutes.

● Line a 39 × 35cm (15¼ × 13¾in) baking sheet with baking parchment. Carefully take the fondant discs, one at a time, and, using two forks, dip in the melted chocolate until coated all over. Be quick about it, you don't want to melt the fondant. Place the coated fondant disc onto the baking parchment. Continue until all the discs are coated. Top each chocolate with a crystallised violet petal and leave to cool and set in a cool place. Place in sweet cases to serve, if you like.

SYRUP SPONGE NUGGETS

with lashings of custard

Syrup sponge served with lashings of vanilla custard is Wingnut's (our 23-year-old son) favourite pudding. So I decided to combine vanilla-laced chocolate with gloopy syrup sponge. I think you will like it, it is certainly an unexpected filling, if a little eccentric; a wonderful cross twixt pudding and chocolate.

Take 20 minutes to make; overnight plus 2 hours in total to cool and set.

100g (4oz) golden syrup
25g (1oz) unsalted butter
100g (4oz) crumbled sponge
   cake (that's 5 shop-bought
   fairy cakes, as it happens)
200g (8oz) white chocolate,
   broken into small bits

For the vanilla chocolate coating
400g (14oz) white chocolate,
   broken into small bits
seeds from 1 vanilla pod
chocolate stars, to decorate
(optional)

✤ Take the golden syrup and whack it in a pan with the butter, then melt gently until the mixture is all runny and oozy. Put the crumbled sponge cake into a bowl and pour the syrup mixture onto it, mixing well until all the syrup has soaked into the sponge. Okay, you can try it. There is no stopping you, is there?

✤ Place 5cm (2in) hot water in a pan and heat until simmering. Pop a heatproof bowl on top of the pan, making sure that the bottom of the bowl is not touching the water. Place the white chocolate in the bowl and very gently warm it until melted. Remove from the heat and set aside to cool, but check to make sure that the chocolate has melted.

✤ Pour the hot chocolate over the syrup sponge and mix together until they are united in a golden marriage of syrup and cakiness. Place in the fridge overnight until the mixture is firm.

✤ Using a teaspoon, take a dollop of the mixture and, using the palms of your hands, roll it into a nugget and drop it onto a clean plate. Continue until you have a plateful of golden nuggets, then return them to the fridge to firm up again.

✤ To make the vanilla chocolate coating, place 5cm (2in) of hot water in a pan and heat. Pop a heatproof bowl on top of the pan, making sure that the bottom of the bowl is not touching the water. Place the chocolate and the seeds scraped from the

➤

vanilla pod into the bowl and gently warm until melted, stirring to distribute the vanilla seeds. Remove from the heat.

❋ Line a 39 × 35cm (15¼ × 13¾in) baking sheet with baking parchment. Carefully take each golden nugget and, using two forks, dip the nugget in the melted chocolate until coated all over. Place the coated nugget on the baking sheet. Leave the nuggets to cool and pop them in the fridge to set. When set, warm the white chocolate once again and coat the nuggets for a second time. Continue until all the nuggets are coated with the chocolate then sprinkle with the chocolate stars, if using. (You will have chocolate left but you need to keep it not eat it!) Leave to cool, serve, stand back and accept the applause.

MATCHA & WHITE CHOCOLATE TRUFFLES

whoo-hoo tangly taste buds

MAKES

14

Matcha is ground green tea; it is pretty much good for everything, including weight loss. Jokes. I have whizzed it with white chocolate and double cream, tossed in a pinch of salt and added a whoo-hoo of tangly taste buds with a wasabi pea. Matcha-slurping is a well-known custom with students in Japan who slurp it to stay alert when revising. Here in Britain students eat instant noodles and wear traffic cones on their heads.

Take 30 minutes to make, plus chilling and freezing.

300g (11oz) white chocolate
2 tbsp double cream
30g (1oz) unsalted butter
1 tsp matcha green tea,
    plus extra for sprinkling
a good pinch of sea salt
wasabi peas

❋ Start by breaking 100g of the chocolate into pieces and put in a heatproof bowl. Rest the bowl over a pan of simmering water, making sure the base doesn't touch the water. Allow to melt.

❋ As soon as it has melted, take off the heat and stir in the cream, butter, matcha green tea and sea salt. Beat well, then cool and chill.

❋ Take a teaspoon and scoop up some of the mixture. Roll into balls then freeze for 30 minutes until as firm as a tightrope walker's thigh. If they've flattened slightly during the chilling, re-roll to shape them into balls.

❋ Temper the remaining chocolate (see page 11) and coat each truffle in the chocolate. Push a wasabi pea on top, drizzle over a little more chocolate and sprinkle with a little matcha and salt. Drizzle a little extra chocolate over the top then chill for 20 minutes to set. Heaven.

MANGO TRUFFLES

slip into your harem pants

MAKES

20

LUCKY TRUFFLES

The mango is considered by many to mean 'good luck'. In order to bring good fortune on yourself, simply prepare my fragrant Mango Truffles. Put on your harem pants, fashion a boob tube from the leaves of the mystical mango tree and do a snake dance on your kitchen table.

Take around 45 minutes to make, plus chilling and overnight freezing.

½ small mango
100g (4oz) white chocolate
2 tbsp double cream
25g (1oz) unsalted butter
175g (6oz) white chocolate, for tempering
1–2 dried mango pieces, chopped into small pieces
a little gold lustre (please see page 186 for stockists)

❦ Scoop about 75g (3oz) of the mango flesh out of its skin. Whizz to a pulp in a mini food processor, or just bash it using a mestal and porter.

❦ Heat 5cm (2in) water in a pan until simmering. Put a heatproof bowl on top of the pan; don't let the bottom of the bowl touch the water. Place the chocolate and cream in the bowl and melt slowly. Do not overheat or you will end up with a fudge island in a sea of melted butter.

❦ Slowly stir in the butter and mango purée until combined and chill for 3–4 hours. Use a teaspoon to scoop up small amounts of the mixture and shape into balls. Open freeze on a baking sheet lined with baking parchment until hard. They might have softened a little so quickly re-shape them into rounds if you need to, then transfer to a freezerproof container, cover, then freeze overnight.

❦ Temper the chocolate (see page 11). Use two forks to dip each mango ball into the white chocolate. Toss gently to coat then lift out and place on a sheet of baking parchment. Use a fork to spike up the chocolate a bit. Put a piece of mango on top of each truffle and put aside for the chocolate to set, then chill. Tickle with gold lustre before serving.

{
AHEM
In the eighteenth and nineteenth centuries, South Asian cows were fed exclusively on mango leaves and thus supplied the yellow colour to make the coveted yellow textile dye, 'Indian Yellow'. Not very mid-century modern is it, darling?
}

MALTED NOUGAT

smells like my childhood

MAKES
25
STICKY PIECES

It is time for bed; I am wearing my new PJs, my hot water bottle is filled, water bubbling over its neck with excitement. A mug of a malty, chocolate drink beckons. The very next morning I set to and create this soft and yielding nougat studded with chocolate-coated honeycomb balls. It smells like my childhood – without the cabbage water and hairspray.

Take 30 minutes to make, plus overnight setting.

a dribble of vegetable oil
400g (14oz) caster sugar
100ml (3½fl oz) clear honey
210ml (7fl oz) liquid glucose
2 large egg whites, at room temperature
50g (2oz) dark chocolate, melted and cooled
40g (1½oz) chocolate malt powder
a good pinch of salt
75g (3oz) chocolate-coated honeycomb balls, plus a few more for you to eat – you know you will

You will also need rice paper to line the tin

Line a 17cm (6¾in) square tin with tin foil and brush all over with a little vegetable oil. Line the base with rice paper.

Put the sugar, honey and liquid glucose in a large, heavy-bottomed pan (I use a deep 24cm (9½in) diameter pan) with 2 tablespoons cold water. Heat gently to dissolve the sugar. Pop a sugar thermometer in the pan and bring the mixture to the boil. Allow to bubble until the temperature reaches 125°C (257°F). Meanwhile, put the egg whites in the bowl of a freestanding mixer and whisk until stiff peaks form, taking care not to overbeat.

When the syrup reaches 125°C (257°F) you need to work quickly. Start the beaters, running on a low setting, then whip out the thermometer and pour half of the syrup in a steady stream onto the egg whites and continue to beat .

Return the pan with the remaining syrup to the heat, pop the thermometer back in and cook until the temperature reaches 157°C (315°F). The mixture should be a dark caramel colour. Pour this mixture into the food mixer, slowly as you go – it will froth up to the top of the mixing bowl. Mix on a moderate speed for a few minutes to incorporate all the syrup. The mixture will thin down after a minute or so.

Add the chocolate, malt powder and salt and mix until incorporated – the mixture will turn a rich nutty brown.

Pour the mixture into the prepared tin, scatter over half the honeycomb balls, then halve the remainder and scatter them over the top. Cool, then leave to set overnight. Cut into squares before serving. Give yourself a round of applause – that was quite a tricky one.

GIN & LIME TRUFFLES

gin 'o' clock

20

Here I have craftily concealed a tipple of gin inside a luscious dark chocolate truffle with a wicked twist of fresh lime. It carries a punch akin to that of Bert Bantam the 8-stone featherweight boxer from Eccles, who unexpectedly knocked out the Giant of Redcar, Mr Arthur Whitlow, at the 1953 Pigeon and Ferret Fanciers Fair with just a single blow to the left buttock.

Take around 30 minutes to make, plus overnight chilling.

100g (4oz) dark chocolate, broken into pieces
2 tbsp double cream
50g (2oz) unsalted butter, chopped
2 tbsp gin
zest and juice of ½ lime
cocoa powder, to dust

❧ Heat 5cm (2in) water in a pan until simmering. Put a heatproof bowl on top of the pan, making sure the bottom of the bowl is not touching the water. Whap the chocolate in the bowl with the cream and heat gently to allow the chocolate to melt. Remove from the heat.

❧ Stir in the butter until you get a smooth, glossy mixture. Tipple in the gin, lime zest and juice and whisk the ingredients together until smooth and slightly thickened. Spoon into a sealable container, snap on the lid and chill overnight.

❧ Take teaspoons of the mixture and roll into balls. Put on a baking sheet lined with baking parchment and chill for an hour or so. *Build a Boat in your Front Room* is on the telly followed by *Divorce on the High Seas.*

❧ Sift the cocoa into a bowl and roll the truffles in it to cover.

❧ Eat them and text ex-boyfriends.

> **HOUSEHOLD USES FOR GIN**
> *Gin is excellent for making things vanish. Simply drink half a bottle and watch irritating husbands and children with maths homework disappear.*

Christopher COLUMBUS

He was set free in 1502 to make a fourth voyage, but failed to find the passage to Asia for which he was seeking. He returned to Spain a disa... to court, and ... man, too sick even to go ... died in poverty in the t... of Valla...

173

CHILLI & LIME KISSES

feel the burn

MAKES
40
FIERY LIPS

History Fact
It is widely accepted that
Christopher Columbus had
a busy year in 1492.

Apparently Christopher Columbus discovered the chilli pepper on one of his travels; I can't remember where he was at the time, somewhere foreign, probably. To celebrate, natives honoured him with palm-leaf platters laden with these fiery, chocolate kisses filled with spicy chilli jam and a twist of lime.

Take 40 minutes to make, plus chilling and setting time.

50g (2oz) dark chocolate, finely chopped
2 tbsp double cream
10g (½oz) unsalted butter, chopped
zest of ½ lime
8 tsp crushed chilli flakes, ground into a powder
a pinch of salt
white chocolate, for tempering

You will also need 2 × 20 lips chocolate moulds (please see page 186 for stockists)

❀ Heat 5cm (2in) water in a pan until simmering. Whack a heatproof bowl on top of the pan, making sure the round bottom of the bowl is not touching the water. Delight the bowl by adding the dark chocolate and cream and warming them languorously until melted. Take the pan off the heat.

❀ Add the butter, lime zest, chilli and salt to the bowl and stir liberally. Set aside to cool a bit.

❀ Temper the white chocolate (see page 11) and use a brush or a teaspoon to coat and line the lip moulds. Use a sharp knife or chocolate scraper to tidy up any sloppy bits around the chocolate. Put the moulds in the fridge to set for around 20 minutes. Turn a sheet, polish the door knob, race a pigeon.

❀ Scoop up a little of the dark chocolate and chilli mixture with a teaspoon and use to fill each lip in the mould. Leave a gap of couple of millimetres (1/8 in) at the top, otherwise there won't be enough space for the chocolate topping. Chill in the fridge for about 20 minutes.

❀ Temper some more white chocolate or use any that's left over from before (but you might need to add some more chocolate to it). Use a teaspoon to fill the moulds, covering all of the dark chocolate and chilli mixture. Chill again until set.

❀ Take the chocolates out of the fridge and upturn onto a board – they should slip out easily – just like the lie you told about Bob. Any that are reluctant to disembark may require a persuasive twist of the mould to release them.

NOUGAT CLUSTERS

as simple as Simple Simon

MAKES

8

WHOPPERS

In this really simple but delightful recipe, crisped rice cereal, creamy milk chocolate, sour cherries, pecans and white nougat are all clustered together in chewy harmony. They are almost as simple as Simple Simon and his Dancing Teeth.

Take 15 minutes to make; plus setting time.

8 pieces white nougat
milk chocolate, for tempering
8 dried soured cherries
8 whole pecan nuts
2 tbsp crisped rice cereal
white chocolate, for tempering

🍫 Put the nougat on a freezerproof plate and slip it into the freezer. Line a board with baking parchment.

🍫 Temper the milk chocolate (see page 11).

🍫 Make 8 dainty piles of the remaining ingredients (except the white chocolate) on the lined board, dividing the crisped rice equally among them so no one gets jealous.

🍫 When the milk chocolate is tempered, remove the nougat from the freezer and pop a piece onto each crispy pile.

🍫 Balance a pile of the ingredients on a dessertspoon and scoop it into the chocolate, making sure all the ingredients are covered. Place the chocolatey cluster on the parchment. Repeat to cover all the piles. Towards the end, you may need to dribble any naked bits the chocolate hasn't covered with the chocolate left in the bowl.

🍫 Allow to set, then temper the white chocolate. Dip a balloon whisk into the white chocolate and drizzle it all over the clusters. Leave to set and enjoy!

TEQUILA CHILLIES

the hokey cokey of confections

MAKES
8
MADLY FABULOUS CHILLIES

You put your chillies in,
Pour tequila out,
In out, in out,
Shake sea salt about.
You add the lime ganache
and you turn around
That's what it's all about . . .

Take 40 minutes to make,
plus 48 hours soaking,
and overnight chilling.

8 mild or spicy fresh
   green chillies
3 tbsp silver tequila
1 tbsp double cream
50g (2oz) white chocolate,
   chopped
zest of ½ lime and a squeeze
   of lime juice
25g (1oz) unsalted butter,
   chopped
white chocolate, for tempering
about 1 tsp flaked sea salt

Don a pair of rubber gloves (otherwise your fingers will sting for days from doing this; anyway you know you love wearing rubber gloves). Cut a slit lengthways down the middle of each chilli and carefully take out the seeds. Put them in a sealable container and add 2 tablespoons of the tequila. Leave to soak for 48 hours – the soaking takes the sting out of the chillies.

Heat 5cm (2in) water in a pan. Pop a heatproof bowl on top of the pan, making sure the bottom of the bowl is not touching the water. Place the cream and chocolate in the bowl. Place over a gentle heat to allow the chocolate to melt.

Take the bowl off the heat and add the remaining tequila, the lime zest and juice and butter. Whisk everything until it becomes a smooth ganache, pour into a sealable container, then chill overnight to set.

When you are ready to fill the chillies, take a teaspoon and scoop up about half a teaspoon of ganache and stuff it into the chillies. Chill.

Temper the white chocolate (see page 11). Dip each chilli in the chocolate to cover, then sprinkle each with a little sea salt. Place the chillies on a baking sheet covered with baking parchment to set.

Sing-a-long
What if the hokey cokey
is really all it's about?

LIMONCELLO CREAMS

zesty limoncello ganache

MAKES
18
DIVINE TRUFFLES

Limoncello is an Italian lemon liqueur made from the Sorrento lemon, which is grown in southern Italy. These white-chocolate creams are filled with a divine zesty limoncello ganache. They are as pure as Katherine Hepburn in Summer Madness *as she leans out from the Venice train, gardenia in hand, waving a tearful goodbye to Rossano Brazzi.*

Take around 40 minutes to make, plus 2 nights chilling and freezing.

100g (4oz) white chocolate
2 tbsp double cream
zest of ½ lemon
1–2 tbsp limoncello liqueur
a pinch of salt
50g (2oz) unsalted butter, chopped
white chocolate, for tempering

Heat 5cm (2in) water in a pan. Put a heatproof bowl on top of the pan, making sure the bottom of the bowl is not touching the water. Place the 100g (4oz) chocolate in the bowl with the cream and heat gently to allow the chocolate to melt.

Take the bowl off the heat and toss in the lemon zest, limoncello, salt and butter and whisk airy fairily until the mixture resembles home-made lemon curd. Try really hard not to make a round of toast. Spoon into a sealable container, put the lid on and chill overnight.

Scoop up small teaspoons of the mixture and roll into balls. Put on a tray lined with baking parchment and freeze overnight.

Temper the white chocolate (see page 11). Use a dipping fork, or two common forks, to dip each truffle into the chocolate. Toss about blithely to coat, then lift out and place back on the parchment, roughening the chocolate with a fork. Repeat, then chill the chocolates to allow them to set.

Tip
Chocolate is usually at its best at room temperature; however, I recommend you eat these almost icy cold – like Rossano Brazzi's heart.

SHERRY
TRIFLE CUPS

Betty Bright's chocolate cup of jelly and Madeira

MAKES

11

BETTY BRIGHT CUPS

My grandfather's diary tells the story of Betty Bright, his first love, who caught his eye when demonstrating her extraordinary unicycle tricks outside the chip shop. Slipped into the back of his diary was Betty's recipe for sherry trifle. I have reworked her original recipe into the most splendidly delicate chocolate 'cup' – with real jelly and Madeira cream.

Take 45 minutes,
plus chilling and setting.

white chocolate, for tempering
2 cubes raspberry jelly
50ml (2fl oz) double cream
a pinch of icing sugar
2 tsp Madeira
hundreds and thousands,
  to decorate

You will also need an
11-hole fluted cup chocolate
mould (please see page
186 for stockists)

❧ Temper the white chocolate (see page 11) and use a clean, grease-free brush or teaspoon to coat and thickly line each of the fluted cups in the mould with the chocolate. Go to it as quick as a stick otherwise the chocolate will cool and become too thick to work with. Use a sharp knife to tidy up any raggedy bits around the chocolate cups. Chill for 20 minutes. Scrape any chocolate that you haven't used into a bowl and save to use again.

❧ Chop up the jelly and put in a bowl with 2 tablespoons of boiling water. Whisk furiously, to melt the jelly, then set aside until cold but not quite set, just a bit wibbly-wobbly.

❧ Take the chocolate cups from the mould by gently upturning onto a board. Then set them the right way up. Spoon the cooled jelly equally among the chocolate cups. Chill to set.

❧ Beat the cream in a bowl until thick, then fold in the icing sugar and Madeira. Spoon the mixture over the jelly-filled cups then sprinkle with hundreds and thousands. Down in one and don't spare the horses.

GARDEN MINT 'PEAS'

*as clean and refreshing
as David Cassidy*

Handy Hint
Counts as one of your five-a-day (and the cheque's in the post).

MAKES

50–60
PEA-SIZED TRUFFLES

When I am out for supper I tend to forego coffee for fresh mint tea – so clean and refreshing. The minty centre to this delicious pea-sized truffle is gentle and subtle, while the crunchy, garden-mint sugar coating makes the pleasure buds along the side of my mouth go all jiggy with anticipation. It is a delight after supper, both cleansing and regenerating, like a walk in the rain with David Cassidy.

Take 30 minutes to make; 3 hours to overnight to cool and set, depending on your patience.

200ml (7fl oz) double cream
25g (1oz) unsalted butter
2 drops of peppermint oil
200g (7oz) dark chocolate,
   broken into small bits
60g (2½oz) garden mint leaves
8 tbsp caster sugar

🌿 Pop the cream and butter into a pan and heat gently, without letting the mixture boil. When it is hot, remove it from the heat and add the 2 drops of peppermint oil; no more, no less.

🌿 Put the broken chocolate into a bowl. Pour the cream over the chopped-up chocolate, give it a brisk stir and set it aside, but check it to make sure the chocolate has melted.

🌿 Cool the mixture in the fridge until firm; overnight is best.

🌿 Line a 39 × 35cm (15¼ × 13¾in) baking sheet with baking parchment. Using a teaspoon, take a pea-sized amount of the mixture, roll it into a ball and drop it onto the baking sheet. Repeat until all the mixture is rolled into 'peas', then set aside.

🌿 Place the mint leaves and caster sugar into a mortar and pestle (you may need to do this in batches) and bash it up, as if it were your ex, until the mint and sugar are combined in a fragrant emerald-green sherbet.

🌿 Roll the truffle peas in the mint sugar until they are coated all over, pressing the minty sugar into the 'peas' as you go. Place on the baking sheet and leave in a cool place.

ROSEHIP
ICED GEMS

on doctor's orders

MAKES
30
LITTLE MERINGUES

For an age I've wanted to create a treat with rosehip – that natural vitamin C syrup that nursed the sniffles of my childhood. So here are some tiny little meringue gems laced with rosehip syrup and dipped in crystallised rose petals. I also liked those tiny orange aspirin nestling under a wad of cotton wool, gargling with antiseptic and the smell of an elastic bandage. Now it's more chapstick, gin and magic pants.

Take around 2 hours 15 minutes to make.

1 medium egg white
50g (2oz) caster sugar
pink food colouring paste
50g (2oz) white chocolate
½ tsp rosehip syrup (please
   see page 186 for stockists)
1–2 tbsp crystallised rose petals

You will also need a piping bag and size 30 star nozzle

❀ Preheat the oven to 110°C/225°F/Gas ¼. Line a large baking sheet with baking parchment. Fit the piping bag with the nozzle.

❀ Whisk the egg white in a spotlessly clean greasefree bowl until as stiff as a stalk and it clings to the side of the bowl. It should be so steady that you can hold the bowl upside down over your head and nothing will slip out. Send photos.

❀ Continue to whisk, adding the sugar a tablespoon at a time until the sugar has dissolved in the mixture.

❀ Add a dot or two of pink food colouring paste to the bowl with a skewer. Fold very roughly, rough is good, into the meringue. Spoon into the piping bag.

❀ Dot a little meringue on the back of each corner of the parchment and press down to secure. Pipe little meringues onto the parchment, working quickly and evenly.

❀ Bake the meringues in the oven for 1 hour 40 minutes until you can lift one easily from the parchment. Then allow to cool.

❀ Melt the chocolate in a bowl resting over a pan of simmering water, making sure the base doesn't touch the water. Fold in the rosehip syrup. Whizz the rose petals in a mini food processor, until roughly chopped, or use a knife. Spread the base of each meringue with a little chocolate then dip in the chopped crystallised rose petals. Allow to set then serve.

DEVON STRAWBERRY TRUFFLES

a little homage to the Devonshire tea

MAKES

18

STRAWBERRY TREATS

As a little homage to the Devonshire tea, my truffles are filled with a milk chocolate strawberry ganache and covered in white chocolate. If you've not tried a Devonshire tea, please do pop into my house any day between 3pm and 5pm and I will rustle up some warm scones, clotted cream and strawberry jam. How much love can one woman give?

Take 40 minutes to make, plus overnight chilling and 4 hours freezing.

100g (4oz) milk chocolate, broken into pieces
1 tbsp double cream
25g (1oz) unsalted butter, chopped
2 tbsp strawberry liqueur
white chocolate, for tempering
18 dried strawberries

Heat 5cm (2in) water in a pan. Pop a heatproof bowl on top of the pan, making sure the bottom of the bowl is not touching the water. Place the chocolate and cream in the bowl and let the chocolate melt over a gentle heat.

Remove from the heat, add the butter and liqueur to the bowl and stir. A little whisk is really handy to beat everything together here; you may be tempted to use your tongue, but remember, Father Christmas is watching. Spoon into a sealable container and chill overnight to set.

Line a 39 × 35cm (15¼ × 13¾in) baking sheet with baking parchment. Take teaspoons of the mixture and roll it into balls. Place them on the baking sheet and freeze for at least 4 hours until as hard as Big Bunty the Muscleman's Daughter.

Temper the white chocolate (see page 11). Use a dipping fork, or two small forks, to drop the truffles into the chocolate and toss to coat. Lift out and place on the baking parchment. Top with a dried strawberry immediately, before the chocolate sets.

Cream Tea Etiquette
Cornish cream tea – the strawberry jam goes on the scone before the cream. Devonshire tea – the strawberry jam goes on top of the cream.

CHILLI & LIME SHARDS

for people with 50 wives

MAKES

10

SPICY SHARDS

My friend Betty is taking her hubby on holiday to Mexico. When I told her that Montezuma drank 50 cups of chilli hot chocolate a day, one for each of his 50 wives, she looked up from her ironing, got all giddy and wistful and lightly spray-starched her antimacassar.

Take 20 minutes to make; cool and set overnight.

400g (14oz) dark chocolate, broken into small bits
finely grated zest of 2 limes
2 tsp chilli flakes, to taste
½ tsp sea salt

🍫 Temper the chocolate (see page 11).
🍫 Add the lime zest, half the chilli flakes and the sea salt. Stir until they are evenly distributed.
🍫 Pour the spicy chocolate onto a 39 × 35cm (15¼ × 13¾in) baking sheet lined with baking parchment and scatter the remaining chilli flakes over the top. Leave in a cool place to set – overnight is best. Once set, break lengthways into uneven shards and serve.

Handy Hint
Place a scoop of good chocolate ice cream between two shards for a spicy twist on a classic choc ice.

CHAPTER
№3
FRUITY

TWINKLY BLACKCURRANT FLOWERS

a simple recipe for children

Children across the land will love to make this simple recipe. Cheer as fondant is squished into the shag pile and weep tears of joy as you spray stain remover on the sofa. I have used the blackcurrant drink of my youth, which I always drank hot after school with a square orange and Josie and the Pussycats.

Take 15 minutes to make; 1 hour to set.

2 tbsp double cream
3 tbsp blackcurrant cordial (undiluted)
275g (10oz) fondant icing sugar, plus extra for rolling
silver balls, to decorate
pink iridescent edible glitter, to decorate

You will also need a small flower biscuit cutter (or a heart or butterfly would be pretty too) and a few children who like all things twinkly and pink

✿ Pour the cream and cordial into a large bowl and mix well.

✿ Sift the icing sugar over the cream mixture and stir to combine. Knead until it resembles bread dough – this only takes about 1 minute and children will love getting stuck in. If the fondant seems a little runny, just add some more icing sugar until it feels like elasticated bread dough.

✿ Wrap the fondant in cling film and pop in the fridge for 30 minutes to firm up.

✿ Place a sheet of cling film on your worksurface and dust with icing sugar. Put the ball of fondant on top. Place another piece of cling film on top of the fondant. Using a rolling pin, roll out the fondant until it is about 1cm (½in) deep. Cut the fondant into shapes using the biscuit cutter and place on a 39 × 35cm (15¼ × 13¾in) baking sheet. Press a silver ball into the centre of each flower and sprinkle with pink iridescent edible glitter. Set aside until firm.

✿ The fondants will last about a week if stored in an airtight container.

FIG & CASSIS TRUFFLES

Cleopatra's fave truffle

MAKES
20
FIG-SHAPED TRUFFLES

My fabulous fig-shaped truffles are made from luscious figs, milk chocolate, a splash of cassis and then rolled in purple sugar.

Take 25 minutes to make, plus chilling and setting time.

6 dried figs, chopped
3 tbsp crème de cassis
200g (7oz) milk chocolate
2 tbsp double cream
50g (2oz) unsalted butter
caster sugar, to dust
a few drops of purple food colouring (or mix together blue and red)

20 sweet cases (optional)

❧ Introduce the figs to the pan, slosh in the cassis and bring to the boil, then simmer for 1 minute. Cool them. Tum te tum. Whizz with abandon into a sumptuous purée – don't worry if there are a few pieces of fig skin, there's nothing wrong with chunky (as my mother used to say).

❧ Heat 5cm (2in) water in a pan until simmering. Pop a heatproof bowl on top of the pan, making sure the bottom of the bowl is not touching the water. Allow the chocolate and cream to mingle in the bowl until warm and melted – don't stir it otherwise it may turn into a right disaster. Stir in the butter. Stir in the fig purée then cover and chill for at least 2 hours until as firm as a builder's arm.

❧ Sprinkle a couple of tablespoons of caster sugar onto a plate, add a couple of drops of food colouring and rub in with your fingers to colour the sugar.

❧ Take a meaningful teaspoonful of the chocolate fig mixture and roll it around between willing palms until all your balls are perky. Shape the mixture, pulling it upwards to make a fig shape. Repeat with the rest of the mixture to make around 20 fig-shaped truffles.

❧ Roll each truffle in the coloured caster sugar to coat. Present them in paper cases if you wish and chill until stiff.

> **SWEET TRIVIA**
> *Rumour has it that Cleopatra hid her asp in a basket of figs. It was she who, on her death bed, gasped the immortal line, 'Does my asp look big in this toga?'*

TOFFEE APPLES

with liquorice root 'stalks'

I am a real stickler for traditional Hallowe'en fare, such as these sticky toffee apples with liquorice root 'stalks'. A walk in The Oak Wood is not complete without a warm pocket of buttery bonfire toffee, ginger beer and the odd soul cake. The word Hallowe'en is short for All Hallows' Eve, and if you spell Hallowe'en without the apostrophe I will get really quite cross with you.

Take 30 minutes to make, plus cooling time.

6 small English knobbly
    apples
butter, for greasing

For the toffee
200g (7oz) granulated sugar
100ml (4fl oz) cold water
1 tsp white wine vinegar
125ml (4½fl oz) golden syrup
25g (1oz) unsalted butter

You will also need 6 liquorice root sticks, or 6 wooden lolly sticks (or indeed get out in the garden and acquire 6 reasonably sturdy twigs – not poisonous ones – complete with the odd leaf or two)

❁ Wash the apples and pop them into the fridge for a couple of hours; this will help the toffee stick to the apple.

❁ Lightly grease a 39 × 35cm (15¼ × 13¾in) baking sheet.

❁ Put the sugar into a large, heavy-bottomed pan with the water. Heat gently for 5 minutes until the sugar has dissolved. Stir with a wooden spoon occasionally and check for any remaining sugar crystals on the back of a metal spoon.

❁ Add the vinegar, golden syrup and butter. Put a sugar thermometer in the pan and bring to a gentle boil on a medium heat. Bubble away until the thermometer reaches 127°C (260°F). This may take up to 30 minutes but don't be tempted to whack the heat up or the toffee will burn in an instant, your smoke alarm will go off and you will have to flap about with a tea towel.

❁ While you are waiting for the caramel to reach the correct temperature, whittle the end of your sticks to a point. Push one stick firmly into the stalk end of each apple. Fill the sink with cold water.

❁ Remove the caramel from the heat and dip the base of the pan in the sink. Pick up the first apple by its stick and dip it into the caramel to coat completely, turning it round, humming a little tune about elves and bonfires.

❁ Place the apple, bum-side down, on the baking sheet and leave to cool. Repeat with the remaining apples.

VARIATION – NUTTY TOFFEE APPLES

Add a handful of chopped nuts to the toffee before dipping the apple into it.

CANDIED PEELS

a frost of sugar crystals

MAKES

25

STRIPS OF SUGARED
PLEASURE

Candied peel is everything good; it is sparkling with a frost of sugar crystals, full of citrus feel-good aromas and tastes jolly fine into the bargain. Oh, how green with envy will Brenda be when you pop round with a cake enriched with your very own home-made candied peel.

Take about 50 minutes to make; about 4 hours in total to cool and set.

2 unwaxed oranges
75g (3oz) granulated sugar
1 vanilla pod
175ml (6fl oz) water
caster sugar, for dusting
100g (4oz) milk chocolate,
    for tempering
1 tsp groundnut oil

LET'S START WITH ORANGE PEEL

❋ Peel the oranges carefully, leaving as much bitter white pith attached to the orange as you can. Cut the peel lengthways into strips about 5mm (¼in) thick.

❋ Put the peel into a small, deep pan and add enough cold water to just cover the peel. Bring the water to the boil, drain and refill with the same amount of cold water again. Bring to the boil and repeat twice (so three times in total). This takes about 30 minutes. Lean an elbow on your worktop and while away several minutes watching it boil.

❋ After the final draining, add the sugar and vanilla to the pan of peel with the water. Over a gentle heat, stir until the sugar has dissolved and then bring to the boil until the peel is soft and yielding, about 10 minutes. It smells fantastic. Remove the peel from the heat and leave to cool.

❋ Drain off any syrup (there may not be much depending on how much has evaporated), then lay the strips out on a wire rack for 24–48 hours, until completely dry. Dip each strip of peel into a bowl of caster sugar, coating it evenly all over. Place on a wire rack to become crisp and sugar crusted.

❋ Temper the chocolate (see page 11).

❋ Half-dip each piece of peel in the chocolate and place on a sheet of baking parchment to set.

2 unwaxed lemons
100g (4oz) granulated sugar
125ml (4½fl oz) water
caster sugar, for dusting
100g (4oz) dark chocolate,
  broken into small pieces
1 tsp groundnut oil

NOW YOU CAN TRY LUSCIOUS LEMON PEEL

🌸 Peel the lemons carefully, leaving as much bitter white pith attached to the lemon as you can. Cut the peel lengthways into strips about 5mm (¼in) thick.

🌸 Put the peel into a small, deep saucepan; add enough cold water to just cover the peel. Bring the water to the boil, drain and refill with the same amount of cold water again. Bring to the boil and repeat twice (so three times in total). This takes about 30 minutes.

🌸 After the final draining, add the sugar to the pan of peel with the water. Over a gentle heat, stir until the sugar has dissolved and then bring to the boil until the peel is soft and yielding, about 10 minutes. Remove from the heat and leave to cool.

🌸 Drain off any syrup (there may not be much depending on how much has evaporated), then lay the strips out on a wire rack for 24–48 hours, until completely dry. Dip each strip of peel into a bowl of caster sugar, coating it evenly all over. Place on a wire rack to become crisp and sugar crusted.

🌸 Temper the chocolate (see page 11).

🌸 Half-dip each piece of peel in the chocolate and place on a sheet of baking parchment to set.

1 unwaxed grapefruit
75g (3oz) granulated sugar
175ml (6fl oz) water
caster sugar, for dusting
100g (4oz) white chocolate,
    broken into small pieces

... OR ZESTY GRAPEFRUIT

● Peel the grapefruit carefully, leaving as much bitter white pith attached to the grapefruit as you can. Cut the peel lengthways into strips about 5mm (¼in) thick.

● Put the peel into a small, deep pan; add enough cold water to just cover the peel. Bring the water to the boil, drain and refill with the same amount of cold water again. Bring to the boil and repeat twice (so three times in total). This takes about 30 minutes.

● After the final draining, add the sugar to the pan of peel with the water. Over a gentle heat, stir until the sugar has dissolved and then bring to the boil until the peel is soft and yielding, about 10 minutes. Remove the peel from the heat and leave to cool.

● Drain off any syrup (there may not be much depending on how much has evaporated), then lay the strips out on a wire rack for 24–48 hours, until completely dry. Dip each strip of peel into a bowl of caster sugar, coating it evenly all over. Place on a wire rack to become crisp and sugar crusted.

● Temper the chocolate (see page 11).

● Half-dip each piece of peel in the chocolate and place on a sheet of baking parchment to set.

PEACH & APRICOT PASTILLES

little jellies twinkling like sugary jewels

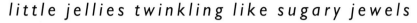

MAKES

30

FIRM JELLIES

Handy Hint
Once you have mastered peaches and apricots, experiment with other fruits such as dried strawberries or pears.

Mr Greenwood loves my wobbly jellies, and who can blame him? In Latin, apricot means 'precious', and indeed these sweet little jellies twinkle away like sugary jewels. Full of luscious apricots and peaches, the jellies are made with pectin, which can be found in the sugar aisle in your supermarket.

Take 45 minutes to make; set overnight.

a little vegetable oil, for greasing
125g (4½oz) no-soak dried peaches
200g (7oz) no-soak dried apricots
475g (1lb 1oz) granulated sugar, plus extra for coating
3 tbsp lemon juice
2 tbsp liquid pectin
2 gelatine leaves

● Line a 20cm (8in) square baking tin with baking parchment and grease it with oil.
● Place the fruit in a pan and cover with 250ml (9fl oz) of water. Cover with a lid and put over a moderate heat, bring to a simmer, then simmer for 15 minutes until the fruit has softened.
● Pop the fruit in a food processor and whizz until well puréed, with no lumps.
● Place the purée, sugar and lemon juice into a deep pan with 100ml (3½fl oz) of water and the lemon juice and heat until the sugar has dissolved. Put a sugar thermometer into the pan, bring to the boil then bring the mixture very slowly up to 107°C (225°F). This will take a good 30 minutes. Take the pan off the heat and pour in the pectin.
● Soak the gelatine leaves in a bowl of cold water.
● Put the pan back on the heat and bring the temperature steadily back up to 110°C (230°F), stirring every now and then.
● Take the pan off the heat, lift the gelatine leaves out of the water and stir in – it will bubble up the pan (that's the fun bit), but give it a good stir.
● Pour the jelly into the prepared tin and leave to cool and set overnight. Once set, turn out onto a board, cut into squares and coat with granulated sugar.
● The pastilles will last for 2–3 days and should be kept in the fridge.

MAPLE WALNUT PEARS

for the rustly-leaf autumn months

MAKES
6
STICKY PEARS

If you like toffee apples but are somewhat fickle, try these hopeylicious maple walnut pears. The pears are coated in a golden toffee, laced with sticky maple syrup and studded with walnuts. They are perfectly joyous in the autumn months, especially with a crackling bonfire and a flagon of spiced cider.

Take 30 minutes to make; a couple of hours to cool.

6 small, ripe dessert pears
butter, for greasing

For the maple toffee
200g (7oz) golden
　　granulated sugar
1 tsp white wine vinegar
125ml (4½fl oz) maple syrup
25g (1oz) unsalted butter
100g (4oz) walnuts, finely
　　chopped

You will also need 6 liquorice root sticks (or 6 wooden lolly sticks)

🌰 Wash the pears and pop them in the fridge for a couple of hours; this will help the toffee stick to the pears.

🌰 Lightly grease a 39 × 35cm (15¼ × 13¾in) baking sheet.

🌰 For the maple toffee, put the sugar into a large, heavy-bottomed pan with 100ml (4fl oz) of water. Warm it gently for 5 minutes until the sugar has dissolved; it should turn a lovely golden brown.

🌰 Add the vinegar, maple syrup and butter. Put a sugar thermometer into the pan and bring the mixture to a gentle boil on a medium heat. Boil until the mixture reaches 127°C (260°F). This may take up to 30 minutes, but don't be tempted to increase the heat or the toffee will burn.

🌰 While you wait, whittle the end of your sticks to a point. Pull the stalk out of each pear, then push one stick firmly into place. Level the bottom of each pear by slicing a little off the base so it sits upright.

🌰 Remove the toffee from the heat. Pick up the first pear by its stick and dip it into the toffee to half-coat it, turning it round and round while humming a little tune about hedgehogs and wood goblins.

🌰 Dip into the chopped walnuts to coat completely, then stand on the baking sheet. Repeat with the remaining pears, then leave to cool.

RASPBERRY MARSHMALLOWS

the weight-loss mallow

MAKES
25
CUBES

I had the enormous pleasure of making this truly delicious, fresh raspberry-studded, sticky, fluffy marshmallow for my friends at my Hip and Thigh exercise class. The ladies there were so excited they fashioned me a throne out of slimmers' crackers and crowned me with a vanilla and chocolate zero-per-cent-lard yoghurt with sprinkles.

Take about 1 hour to make; 2 hours to set, plus 2–3 hours to cool.

icing sugar, to dust
cornflour, to dust
450g (1lb) granulated sugar
1 tbsp liquid glucose
4 gelatine leaves
2 large egg whites

For the raspberry coulis
300g (11oz) fresh raspberries
2 tbsp caster sugar

❀ Line a 20cm (8in) square baking tin (4cm/1½in deep) with baking parchment and, using a sieve, shake equal amounts of icing sugar and cornflour over the base until the parchment is lightly dusted.

❀ First, make the raspberry coulis. Place 100g (4oz) of the fresh raspberries in a pan with the caster sugar (set the remainder aside for decoration later). Cook on a medium heat for around 5 minutes, stirring until it is a lovely ruby-red mush. Strain the mixture into a clean bowl, pressing the pulp through a sieve with the back of a metal spoon. Leave to cool.

❀ Put the sugar, glucose and 200ml (7fl oz) of water into a heavy-bottomed pan and give it a quick stir. Heat gently for about 5–8 minutes to dissolve the sugar. Once the sugar has dissolved, place your sugar thermometer in the pan, bring the liquid to a gentle boil and continue cooking for about 15 long minutes until the mixture reaches 127°C (260°F).

❀ While you are waiting, put the gelatine leaves into a small bowl of water to soften. When the temperature reaches 115–120°C (239–248°F) on the thermometer, start to whisk the egg whites in your food mixer or with an electric hand whisk until just stiff.

❀ When the syrup reaches the correct temperature, remove the pan from the heat and remove the thermometer. Squeeze any excess water from the gelatine and drop the leaves into the syrup. Give it a quick stir with a large metal spoon. Be careful – it will bubble and spit a little and rise to the top of the pan – it is extremely hot.

❀ With the motor still running or still whisking, slowly add the syrup mixture to the eggs. Then on a medium–fast setting, whisk for a further 15 minutes until the mixture is thick, shiny and holding its shape reasonably well on the whisk.

❀ Using a spoon, gently fold the raspberry coulis through the mallow mixture to create a rippled effect. Spoon half the mallow mixture into the dusted tin and place half the reserved raspberries over the top. Spoon the remainder of the mallow mix over the top of the fresh raspberries, smoothing the top with a palette knife if necessary, then scatter the remaining raspberries over the top.

❀ Leave the mallow to set for about 2 hours. Dust a second piece of parchment with icing sugar and cornflour. Turn the mallow out onto the paper. Cut into squares using a knife dipped in hot boiled water, dust the cut edges and leave to dry on a wire rack.

Handy Hint
Make a white chocolate dipping sauce to go with this. Melt 200g (7oz) of white chocolate in a heatproof bowl over a pan of simmering water, pour into a clean bowl and dip away.

PASSION FRUIT HEARTS

call the fire brigade

MAKES
24
AMOROUS HEARTS

Mr Greenwood is often distracted by the fleeting glimpse of a lady's ankle while promenading. My sweet Passion Fruit Hearts are equally tempting and I find myself hiding them in case he gets too giddy.

Take about 30 minutes to make, plus chilling and setting time.

2 passion fruits
25g (1oz) white chocolate, chopped
1 tbsp double cream
5g (¼oz) unsalted butter
white chocolate, for tempering

You will also need 2 chocolate mould trays of 12 bite-sized hearts (please see page 186 for stockists)

🍧 Halve the passion fruits and scoop the juice and seeds into a sieve set over a bowl to the tune of 'Once I had a Secret Love'. Use a wooden spoon to stir the seeds round the sieve to push through the juice and any bits of pulp. Throw away the seeds.

🍧 Heat 5cm (2in) water in a pan. Plonk a heatproof bowl on top of the pan, making sure the bottom of the bowl is not touching the water. Place the 25g (1oz) of white chocolate with the cream in the bowl and warm tenderly until melted. Remove the bowl from the pan and stir the butter and passion fruit juice into the melted chocolate. Whack it on the windowsill for a bit.

🍧 Temper the white chocolate (see page 11) and use a clean, grease-free brush or teaspoon to thinly coat and line the moulds with white chocolate. Please do it faster, you are far too slow; if you don't get a move on the chocolate will cool and become thick. If you are obsessive–compulsive take a sharp knife or chocolate scraper to tidy up any bits around the chocolate hearts. Scrape any white chocolate that you haven't used into a bowl and save to use again. Put the moulds in the fridge to set for around 20 minutes.

🍧 Take the moulds out of the fridge. Spoon a little of the passion-fruit mixture into each heart-shaped mould, leaving a couple of millimetres (⅛in) at the top so there's room to enclose the filling with a layer of white chocolate. Whap

➤→

back in the fridge to set for about 45 minutes. While you wait, go to the spare room window and check if Jean is sunbathing.
🌸 Temper some more white chocolate or use any that's left over from earlier (but you might need to add a little more chocolate to it), and, using a teaspoon, cover all of the passion fruit mixture and fill up the moulds. Chill again to set the chocolate.
🌸 Take the chocolates out of the fridge and upturn the mould trays onto a board – the Passion Fruit Hearts should slip out easily. Any left behind might need a gentle twist of the mould to release them or coaxing out with the promise of a gin and tonic.

SOUR LEMON TRAVEL SWEETS

for placating sisters

MAKES

22
LITTLE DROPS

My little sis' once fell over right in front of the Sisters of Mercy Convent. The shame. She was placated with tiny lemon drops from the chemist and a bottle of cream soda.

Take 30 minutes to make.

a little vegetable oil
icing sugar
125g (4½oz) caster sugar
¼ tsp cream of tartar
75ml (2½fl oz) water
1 tsp powdered citric acid
  (from the chemist)
grated zest of ½ lemon
2 tsp lemon juice

You will also need a silicone, non-slip heat-resistant mat and a baking scraper (see page 186 for stockists)

Oil the mat, scraper and a table knife with vegetable oil. Fill the sink with cold water. Put a couple of tablespoons of icing sugar into a shallow bowl.

Put the sugar, cream of tartar and water in a small, heavy-bottomed pan. Heat gently to dissolve the sugar.

Pop a sugar thermometer into the pan and increase the heat slightly. Allow the mixture to come steadily to the boil and watch it carefully as it climbs to 150°C (300°F).

Take the pan off the heat quickly and plunge the base into the cold water in the sink. Add the citric acid, lemon zest and juice to the pan and stir in.

Pour the hot mixture onto the oiled mat and immediately start working it, teasing it in from each side and folding it into the middle. Continue to do this until the mixture has thickened and cooled considerably. From a big pool of runny liquid, it will look more like a mound of sticky sugar on the mat at this stage.

Take the knife and cut off small pieces. Quickly roll each one into a ball in the palm of your hands and drop into the icing sugar. At this point the mixture will be as warm as a warm hot water bottle and not too hot to handle. Toss well, then put on a plate to cool. Work quickly until you've made 22 sweets.

Once the sweets are cool, tip the icing sugar into a small tin, add the sweets and seal with the lid.

PAVLOVA ISLANDS

*a sweet pirouette of
froth and nonsense*

MAKES
25
WHITE-CHOCOLATE
MERINGUE CHUNKS

*My grandmother will tell
you that she once toured with
Anna Pavlova and was at
dinner when the chef at the
Wellington Hotel presented
Anna with the very first fruit-
filled meringue that came to
be known as a 'Pavlova'. She
will also tell you that the moon
is a great big silver sixpence
and that the people next
door stole her telly.*

Take 20 minutes to make;
cool and set overnight.

800g (1lb 12oz) white
   chocolate, broken into
   small pieces
100g (4oz) meringue
   (about 4 nests)
200g (7oz) dried cherries
   and berries

❃ Line a 20cm (8in) square baking tin (4cm/1½in deep)
with cling film.

❃ Place 5cm (2in) water in a pan and heat. Pop a heatproof
bowl on top of the pan, making sure that the bottom of the
bowl is not touching the water. Place the chocolate in the
bowl and gently warm it to melt. Remove from the heat
and leave to cool for 10 minutes.

❃ Crumble the meringue nests roughly, setting aside
a generous handful of crumble for the decoration.

❃ Mix the cherries and berries into the melted chocolate
then stir in the crumbled meringue. Dollop all the mixture
into the lined tin so it fills the tin but is nice and lumpy.
Top this with the reserved meringue pieces, pressing them
down to make sure they stick to the surface of the chocolate.

❃ Set aside until cold (overnight is best) and then break
into chunks.

Handy Hint
*If your neighbour
has stolen your telly,
put the radio on.*

BLACKBERRY CUPS

Mr Dandy's amuse-bouche

MAKES
11
TOLERABLE MORSELS

*'Despite inclement weather,'
declared Elizabeth Bonnet,
'my sisters and I have plundered
the hedgerows of Wetherfield
Park and devised some tasty
Blackberry Chocolates.'*

*'Surely,' cried Mrs Bonnet,
'these agreeable treats will
suffice to see my Lizzy settled
at Mr Dandy's estate with £50
a year, a plasma screen, and
a drawer full of pizza menus.'*

Take 20 minutes to make,
plus chilling and setting time.

milk chocolate, for tempering
1½ tbsp blackberry jam
1 tbsp crème de cassis
40g (1½oz) white chocolate
1 tbsp double cream
1 vanilla pod
20g (¾oz) unsalted butter
1 sponge finger, crushed
1 tbsp flaked almonds, toasted
   and roughly chopped
a little icing sugar, to dust

You will also need an 11-hole
fluted cup chocolate mould
(see page 186 for stockists)

Temper the milk chocolate (see page 11) and use a clean, grease-free brush or teaspoon to coat and line each of the fluted cups in the mould with the chocolate. You may wish to act hastily as the chocolate will set quickly. Use a chocolate scraper or a knife to scrape away any chocolate from the top of the mould. Scrape any chocolate that you haven't used into a bowl and save to use again. Put the moulds in the fridge to set for around 20 minutes – you may use the time to sew some spotted muslin or to pick out some gay ribbons for the Wetherfield Ball.

Put the blackberry jam and crème de cassis in a pan and heat gently. Stir together. Wander aimlessly to the window licking the spoon timidly. Is that Mr Dandy cantering across The Park?

Heat 5cm (2in) water in a pan. Pop a heatproof bowl on top of the pan, making sure the base is not touching the water. Melt the white chocolate and cream, allowing yourself a fleeting moment to daydream of Mr Dandy. Remove from the heat.

Split the vanilla pod lengthways and run the tip of a knife down the pod to extract the seeds. Chop the butter, add both to the bowl and stir everything together. Resist licking the spoon.

Remove the chocolate cups from the mould by upturning them gently onto a board. Set them the right way up, then divide the boozy jam mix equally among the cups. Dollop with the white chocolate ganache.

Mix the crushed sponge finger with the almonds and divide equally among the cups. Allow to set by chilling for at least 30 minutes, then dust with icing sugar. Let us hope that Mr Dandy finds them tolerable and handsome enough to tempt him.

STRAWBERRY & CREAM LOLLIES

a postcard-perfect Cornish treat

MAKES
4
LIFE- AFFIRMING LOLLIES

Along the windy, sun-kissed lanes of Cornwall, my head scarf is doing an Isadora Duncan and bluebirds chirrup a greeting overhead, when a sign for strawberry cream tea tempts me off road. Here is a postcard-perfect Cornish tearoom with pixies riding on snails, tamed Baskerville Hounds frolicking in ponds of creamed rice and where Agatha Christie is supping cider from a wishing well made entirely of fudge. Then I wake up and remember it is bin day.

Take 15 minutes to make, plus setting.

200g milk chocolate,
   for tempering
25g (1oz) white chocolate
about 12 freeze-dried
   strawberries

You will also need 4 wooden lolly sticks (see page 186 for stockists)

❀ Temper the milk chocolate (see page 11).

❀ Heat 5cm (2in) water in a pan. Place a heatproof bowl on top of the pan, making sure the bottom of the bowl is not touching the water. Slap the white chocolate in the bowl and allow it to melt slowly.

❀ Line a 39 × 35cm (15¼ × 13¾in) baking sheet with baking parchment. Use a 6cm (2½in) round cutter, baked bean tin or mug to draw four circles spaced apart on the parchment, add a smiley face, then turn it over so the ink is underneath. Spoon a pool of milk chocolate onto each circle to fill each round. Place a lolly stick at the bottom of each, then spoon over a little more chocolate. When the chocolate dries the stick will be securely set, yes it will, honest injuns.

❀ Decorate the lollies with three perfectly positioned dried strawberries, then use a teaspoon to blob the white chocolate over the strawberries. Leave them to set, that is the rule.

PEAR & GINGER COINS

treats from the good ol' days

MAKES

A COUPLE OF PURSES

In the good old days farmers' wives would throw a sack around their shoulders and make the 60-mile pilgrimage to market. Ploughing through rain and snow, over hills and down dales, they clutched a precious little leather purse of these fiery baked Conference pear and ginger coins as payment for essential household goods such as mackerel candles, pig soap and donkey cheese. I'm not convinced the good old days were actually that good.

Take 15 minutes to make, plus 3 hours to bake.

2 large Conference pears
1 tbsp golden caster sugar,
   plus extra to sprinkle
1 tsp ground ginger (or
   use ground cinnamon
   if you prefer)

Preheat the oven to 110°C/225°F/Gas ¼. Line two baking sheets with baking parchment.

Slice the pears really thinly into rounds using a mandolin or very sharp knife.

Lay the pears onto the baking parchment. It doesn't matter if you have to squeeze the rounds to fit them all onto the paper; they shrink as they dry out. Lick your fingers.

Stir together the sugar and ginger, then sprinkle liberally over each piece. Bake in the oven for 3 hours, turning over halfway through.

Put the cooled pears into paper bags. Pour the remaining sugar dusting from the baking sheet into a separate little bag and add a little extra sugar to suit. Fold over the top of the bag so it's all safe and happy. Now simply shake the gingery sugar over the pear crisps.

WILD BERRY JELLIES

with permission from Squirrel Greenwood's mum

MAKES

100

LITTLE WOBBLY SQUARES

Once upon a time when the weather had a snap in it and the autumn leaves were trembling on the trees Squirrel Greenwood took his wicker basket, threw a red scarf around his neck and set off to the woods to collect berries for his mummy's sugared, fruit-filled Wild Berry Jellies. He loves his mummy.

Take 40 minutes to make, plus 3–4 hours' chilling.

a little vegetable oil,
    for brushing
20g (¾oz) leaf gelatine
500g (1lb 2oz) frozen mixed
    berries, defrosted
275g (10oz) caster sugar
1 tbsp glucose syrup
2 tbsp crème de cassis

To coat the jelly jewels
caster sugar
icing sugar
cornflour

◈ Whip out your pastry brush and paint a 17cm (6¾in) square tin with vegetable oil, then line it with microwave-proof clingfilm and oil again. Oily.

◈ Separate the gelatine leaves then put in a bowl and cover with cold water. Set aside to soak.

◈ Whizz the berries in a food processor to make a purée. Spoon into a sieve resting over a bowl and use a wooden spoon to stir furiously to extract the juice. Discard the seeds left behind. The berry mixture will have reduced and you'll be left with a thick, dry-ish pulp.

◈ Pop the pulp in a pan with the sugar and 4 tablespoons of boiling water. Heat gently to dissolve the sugar then bring to the boil and simmer for 2 minutes.

◈ Lift the soaked gelatine leaves out of the water – they'll feel floppy and soft at this stage – then stir into the berry mixture. Use a slotted spoon to spoon off any scum floating on the top. Cool in the pan for 10 minutes.

◈ Stir the mixture again then transfer to the lined tin. Allow to cool then chill for 3–4 hours until completely set.

◈ Oil a sharp knife and cut the jelly into 1.5cm (½in) squares. Put 1 tablespoon of caster sugar and 1 tablespoon of icing sugar into a shallow bowl then stir in 1 teaspoon of cornflour. Add 10 jelly squares and toss to coat. Continue to coat them, adding more caster, icing sugar and cornflour as necessary, et voilà.

SHERBET LEMON MARSHMALLOWS

for all my lemon-squeezing chums

Handy Hint
If you pop the lemon into the freezer for 10 minutes first, it makes it much easier to grate.

MAKES

25–30
TINGLE-TASTIC CUBES

I was partaking of lady lemonade one day when I had the glorious idea of combining the tingly lemon fizz with the sugary sweetness of marshmallow. A big hit with Sandra, Ethel and Joan from the launderette, I am duty-bound to share this tingly, lemon-sherbet-dipped mallow recipe with all my lemon-squeezing chums.

Take about 1 hour to make; up to 2 hours to set.

icing sugar, to dust
cornflour, to dust
450g (1lb) granulated sugar
1 tbsp liquid glucose
200ml (7fl oz) water
1 sachet of powdered gelatine
finely grated zest and juice
   of 2 lemons
2 large egg whites
2 tsp yellow food colouring
100g (4oz) lemon sherbet
   crystals, to decorate

❋ Line a 20cm (8in) square baking tin (4cm/1½in deep) with baking parchment and, using a sieve, shake icing sugar over the base until the parchment is lightly dusted.

❋ Put the sugar, liquid glucose and 200ml (7fl oz) of water into a large, heavy-bottomed pan and give it a quick stir. Place your sugar thermometer in the pan, bring the liquid to a gentle boil and continue cooking for about 20–30 long minutes until the mixture reaches 127°C (260°F).

❋ While you are waiting, sprinkle the gelatine over 100ml (4fl oz) of hot water (following the packet instructions), making sure it has dissolved properly. Stir in the lemon zest and juice. Set aside.

❋ When the syrup reaches the correct temperature, remove the pan from the heat and remove the thermometer. Pour the dissolved gelatine into the syrup. Be careful, it will bubble and spit and rise to the top of the pan – it is extremely hot.

❋ Using an electric mixer or whisk, whisk the 2 egg whites together until stiff. Still whisking, slowly add the syrup and gelatine mixture to the egg whites. Add the yellow food colouring. Then, with the mixer on super fast, whisk for a further 20–25 minutes until the mixture is thick, shiny and holding its shape reasonably well on the whisk.

❋ Spoon the mallow mixture into the dusted tin and leave it to set for about 2 hours. Dust a second piece of parchment with equal amounts of icing sugar and cornflour. Turn the mallow out onto the paper. Cut into squares using a knife dipped in hot boiled water; press the cut edges into the lemon sherbet crystals and leave to dry on a wire rack.

SHERBET DIPPER

with a dark caramel lemon lollipop

MAKES

4

LOLLIES

Let us hopscotch into the playground of our past. As homage to the sherbet dips of our childhoods here is my recipe for a sharp, lemon peel sherbet and my dark caramel, lemon lollipop. At a recent school reunion I was delighted to find that all my old playmates still have plasters on their glasses, teeth you could open a pop bottle with and rickets.

Takes around 30 minutes to make, plus setting.

For the sherbet
1 lemon
100g (4oz) caster sugar
1 tsp powdered citric acid
  (from the chemist)

For the lollies
a little vegetable oil
150g (5oz) granulated sugar
juice of ½ lemon
1 tbsp liquid glucose

You will also need
4 lolly sticks

Preheat the oven to 150°C/300°F/Gas 2. Use a vegetable peeler to pare the peel from the lemon, leaving as much white pith as possible on the fruit. Put the peelings on a baking sheet and bake for 15–20 minutes until dried out and golden.

Use a glass or jar to draw four 6–7cm (2½ –3in) rounds on a piece of baking parchment . Turn the paper over and put on a heatproof board. Brush the inside of each round with oil.

Allow the peel to cool, then whizz in a mini blender, or use a knife, until finely chopped. Add the caster sugar and citric acid and whizz again briefly to combine.

Fill the sink with cold water. Just do it, ok?

Put the sugar, lemon juice, liquid glucose and 1 tablespoon of boiling water in a small heavy-bottomed pan and heat gently to dissolve the sugar. Put a sugar thermometer into the pan and increase the heat until the syrup is simmering steadily. Watch the temperature carefully and cook until it reaches 150°C (300°F).

Quickly dip the base of the pan into the water in the sink to stop the caramel cooking any further then take a teaspoon and carefully spoon some of it into each round on the parchment. Push in the sticks and spoon some more syrup into each round – it may run outside the circles but the lollies will be all the more lovely for it. Allow the lollies to set then carefully release from the parchment and serve with the sherbet.

ROCK SUGAR STIRRERS

for wiggling and swirling

MAKES

4

Now I'm not going to lie to you (you are not Mr Greenwood); this is a right fiddly recipe and takes a week of relaxation before it blossoms into a thing of beauty and majesty. Once bloomed the stunning rock sugar crystals can be wiggled and swirled into tea or coffee or a cocktail.

Take 1 week to make.

900g (2lb) caster sugar,
   plus extra for dipping
a selection of food colours
   (a different one for each jar)

You will also need
4 long wooden skewers,
jam jars and pegs and
an overdose of patience

* Pour 475ml water into a pan and bring to the boil. As soon as the water is boiling, gradually add the sugar, a tablespoon at a time and stir in to dissolve.
* Continue to add the sugar in this way, waiting for each spoonful to dissolve before adding another. Patience is a virtue. Once all the sugar has dissolved, cool the syrup.
* Dip each skewer in the syrup, covering all but the tip in the syrup, then into some caster sugar to coat. Clip the peg onto the exposed tip and suspend in the jam jars to dry. Allow them to dry for as long as it takes the syrup to cool.
* Take the skewers out of the jars, then pour a dash of food colour into each jar. Divide the syrup between the jars. Give each a stir to dilute the colour. Suspend the skewer in each jar as before.
* After a day or two there'll be a crust on top of each jar. Carefully, break the crust of one and lift out the skewer. Lift out and discard all the crusty sugar on top, then pour the syrup into a clean jar. Rest the peg holding the skewer on top again. Do the same with the other jars.
* Do the same again after a few days if you see sugar crystals forming on anything but the skewer.
* After a week, carefully lift out the skewer and suspend over a clean glass or jar to dry.

CHERRY BAKEWELL SHARDS

contains a barrel of cherry brandy

MAKES

1

BIG, OUTRAGEOUSLY
CALORIFIC PIECE

My favourite cake of all time, the cherry Bakewell, here reformatted into a giant bar of white chocolate with sour dried cherries and almonds, and layered with soft amaretti biscuits soaked in cherry brandy.

Takes 40 minutes to make, plus setting and chilling.

50g (2oz) *amaretti morbidi* (soft amaretti biscuits)
2 tbsp cherry brandy
25g (1oz) flaked almonds
250g (9oz) white chocolate, for tempering
25g (1oz) dried cherries

- Line a shallow 30 × 22cm (12 × 8 ½in) rectangular baking tray with baking parchment.
- Break the amaretti up between your fingers and crumble it into a bowl. Grab a bottle of cherry brandy, take a slug to make sure it's all good then pour it over the amaretti. Stick the bowl on the windowsill to soak.
- Toast the flaked almonds in a dry frying pan until gorgeous and golden.
- Temper the white chocolate (following the method on page 11). As soon as the chocolate is ready, pour about two thirds of it into the baking tray, tipping it round and about to spread the chocolate into a rectangle about 17 × 15cm (6¾ × 6in). Spoon the macerated biscuits on top then pour the rest of the chocolate on top. Like a great big super-duper chocolate sandwich.
- Swirl the chocolate around with a knife to cover the biscuit, then scatter over the flaked almonds and dried cherries, pushing them down into the chocolate.
- Allow to set then chill, break into shards and chunks; there's no need to be polite.

CHAPTER
№ 4

NUTTY

PROPER PEANUT BRITTLE

peanut pushers' toffee

MAKES

20

NUTTY SHARDS

Handy Hint
This is hot, really hot. Don't even think about putting the toffee pan directly onto your kitchen worksurface, it will burn it. I know this from experience.

If you have a spare moment perhaps you could ape (yes, that was a monkey-nut pun) my American chum Mr Tom Miller, who pushed a peanut to the top of Pike's Peak (14,100 feet) using his nose in 4 days, 23 hours, 47 minutes and 3 seconds. Alternatively, you could enjoy peanuts by staying home, making some proper crunchy peanut brittle and watching the telly.

Takes 45 minutes to make; a couple of hours to cool.

groundnut oil, for greasing
350g (12oz) shelled unsalted
   peanuts
400g (14oz) granulated sugar
100g (4oz) soft light brown
   sugar
150ml (5fl oz) golden syrup
100g (4oz) unsalted butter
150ml (5fl oz) water
¼ level tsp bicarbonate of soda

* Preheat the oven to 180°C/350°F/Gas 4. Lightly oil a 20 × 30cm (8 × 12in) toffee tin, 2.5cm (1in) deep.
* Scatter the peanuts onto a baking sheet and place them in the oven for 10 minutes until golden, taking care not to let them burn.
* Pop both sugars, the golden syrup, butter and water into a deep, heavy-bottomed pan and heat gently until the sugar has dissolved.
* Put a sugar thermometer in the pan and bring the mixture to the boil. Boil very gently for at least 30 minutes, probably more, until your sugar thermometer reaches 149°C (300°F). It will seem like forever, but don't be tempted to turn up the heat as the toffee will burn very easily. Be patient – pat your hamster while you wait.
* Chuck in the bicarbonate of soda and roasted peanuts and chuckle with glee as the mixture bubbles up to the top of the pan like Vesuvius. Remove from the heat.
* Carefully pour the toffee into the prepared tin and leave to cool. Once cool attack the toffee with your toffee hammer, breaking it into lumps. If you have not invested in a toffee hammer you will have to stick a screwdriver into it to break it.

MARZIPAN SANDWICHES

hey nonny nonny

Well, here we are in merrie seventeenth-century England dining on that culinary delight, the 'marchpane'. It took an Elizabethan servant 100 years to grind the almonds and sugar required to make this doublet-tightening cake, and many swooned – falling ruff first, into the sticky mixture.

As luck would have it, you probably have a food mixer.

Take 45 minutes to make, plus 1 hour to cool.

400g (14oz) ground almonds
50g (2oz) icing sugar
450g (1lb) granulated sugar
150ml (5fl oz) water
½ tsp cream of tartar
½ tsp almond extract
green food colouring
pink food colouring
50g (2oz) dark chocolate,
    broken into small bits
30 almond slivers, to decorate

❧ Stir the ground almonds and icing sugar together in a bowl then pop into a food mixer.

❧ Place the granulated sugar and water into a heavy-bottomed pan and place it on a low heat. Stir continuously with a wooden spoon until the sugar has dissolved. This may take 5–10 minutes, so please be patient.

❧ Put a sugar thermometer in the pan, bring the mixture to a boil and add the cream of tartar. Bubble gently for around 10–15 minutes until the syrup reaches 115°C (240°F), then remove from the heat.

❧ Turn on the food mixer and gently add the syrup to the ground almonds in a steady shining thread. Add the almond extract and mix well. Leave to cool for 10 minutes then remove the paste from your food mixer and set aside until it is cool enough to handle.

❧ Divide the mixture into three equal lumps.

❧ To lump 1 add a few drops of green food colouring and then knead the paste until it is the pale green of a leprechaun's waistcoat.

❧ To lump 2 add pink food colouring and knead well until it is the colour of a princess's petticoat.

❧ For lump 3, place 5cm (2in) of hot water in a pan and heat. Pop a heatproof bowl on top of the pan, making sure that the

➤→

bottom of the bowl is not touching the water. Place the chocolate in the bowl and gently warm to melt. Take the bowl off the pan, set aside to cool for 5 minutes, then add the melted chocolate to the paste and knead until it is the brown of a squirrel's hankie.

❀ Place each lump between two pieces of cling film then, using a rolling pin, roll them out until they are roughly rectangular, about 13 × 22cm (5 × 9in) and approximately 5mm (1/5in) thick.

❀ Layer one rectangle of paste on top of another to make a sandwich. I favour a green layer, then brown, then pink, but the choice is yours. Run the rolling pin lightly over the marzipan sandwich to squidge the pastes together.

❀ Cut the marzipan into small, even squares and decorate each with a sliver of almond.

Sugar Gossip
Queen Elizabeth snacked on sugary stuff so much that her teeth were black. The crazy ladies in her court followed suit, blackening their teeth and painting their faces white to ape their beloved queen.

PEAR & CHESTNUT TRUFFLES

a chocolate conker nestling in a prickly case

MAKES

8

CHUNKY TRUFFLES

This autumnal truffle is made with an amazing pear vodka and chestnut ganache wrapped in a scarf of green marzipan, and once enrobed with dark chocolate it looks precisely like a chocolate conker nestling in its prickly case. The autumn wind is whipping through the trees, the sun is low and cool, so take a walk in the park, kick up some leaves, fly a kite, feed the ducks and catch a cold.

Take 1 hour to make, plus chilling and overnight setting.

2 dried pears, finely chopped
75ml (3fl oz) pear vodka
4 cooked chestnuts,
    from a packet
100g (4oz) milk chocolate
25g (1oz) unsalted butter
milk chocolate, for tempering
200g (7oz) marzipan
green food colouring
icing sugar, for dusting
dark chocolate, for tempering

❋ Whap the chopped pears in a pan with the pear vodka and bring to the boil. Drink a bit of vodka. Simmer for 2–3 minutes until the fruit is soft and yielding. Slap the fruity vodka into a mini food processor with the chestnuts and whizz to make a sticky purée.

❋ Heat 5cm (2in) water in a pan until simmering. Plop a heatproof bowl on top of the pan, making sure the ample bottom of the bowl is not dipping into the water. Place the 100g (4oz) milk chocolate in the bowl and warm to melt – please don't stir it otherwise it may turn into a great big, thick mess.

❋ Now then, when the chocolate has melted beauticiously, drop in the butter with the chestnut and pear purée and stir as gently as a kitten. Spoon the mixture into a bowl and chill until firm. If only this method worked on thighs.

❋ Use a teaspoon to scoop out some mixture and shape into small balls the size of marbles. Size is everything. Freeze on a baking sheet covered with baking parchment for 30 minutes to 1 hour.

❋ After that time, temper the milk chocolate (see page 11). Line a board with baking parchment, dip each pear and

chestnut ball into the chocolate using a chocolate dipping fork or table fork or somefink, then lift out and plant on the parchment. Whack them in a safe place to set and firm up like Caster Semenya's calves.

* Knead the marzipan lightly on a board, then drip on a couple of dots of green food colouring (rubber gloves may be worn, if you needed an excuse). Work the food colouring into the marzipan until thoroughly mixed through.

* Dust the work surface with icing sugar then roll out half the marzipan to make a rough square. Cut into four, then wrap each square around one of the pear and chestnut balls. Cut out a horizontal leaf-shaped oval in each marzipan ball, using a sharp knife, to reveal a little of the chocolate underneath. Trim each with a knife round the base and press to shape around the chocolate. Repeat with the remaining chocolates and marzipan, then leave to set at room temperature for at least 8 hours or overnight.

* Temper the dark chocolate, as before. Take a chocolate in one hand and a spoon in the other. Spoon the chocolate all over the marzipan, leaving about a 2mm edge around the green marzipan window. Allow the chocolate to go tacky, then take a fork and press and lift it all over to create a spiky finish. Crack on with covering and spiking up the rest. Once 'punked', allow the chocolate to set.

MAPLE SYRUP, PECAN & BACON LOLLY

crunchers only

I am absolutely besotted with the combo of bacon and maple syrup. Besotted. This joyful recipe tickles all my salty and sweet boxes. It's important to embrace crunching not licking to reveal its taste bombs of salty bacon and maple pecan sweetness.

Take 40 minutes to make, plus setting.

a little vegetable oil
1–2 rashers of unsmoked
    streaky bacon
10g (½oz) pecans, toasted
    and chopped
150g (5oz) caster sugar
25g (1oz) golden syrup
2 tbsp maple syrup

You will also need
4 lolly sticks

Fill the kitchen sink with cold water. Weird but stay with me. Heat your grill to high.

Place a sheet of baking parchment on a board, then draw four 6.5cm (2½in) circles on it, spaced apart. Turn the paper over so that the pencil is on the other side. Brush each round with the oil.

Snip the rind off the bacon rashers, then grill until crisp and golden. Cool, then snip into little pieces. Please try not to eat them, though of course you will.

Divide the cooled bacon among the circles, along with the pecan nuts. Position the lollipop sticks near the circle, too.

Put the sugar and 75ml (2½fl oz) water into a high-sided heavy-bottomed pan and heat gently to dissolve the sugar. Add the golden and maple syrups and put a sugar thermometer in too. Turn up the heat slightly and watch carefully until the thermometer reaches 150°C (300°F). Take the pan off the heat and dip the base of the pan in the sink of cold water to stop the mixture cooking any further. Cool for a minute or two, then carefully spoon some of the syrup into each circle over the bacon/pecans. The syrup will run, but will thicken slightly on cooling. Press in the sticks, then continue to spoon the syrup into the circle on top of the first lot of syrup (if the syrup has gone hard, put the pan back over a low heat to soften it again).

Allow to set then carefully lift off the parchment.

COCONUT ICE

*what harm can a drop
of pink really do?*

*There are a million grillion
ways to make coconut ice,
but here is mine. It is soft,
yielding and ultimately chewy.
Better still, you don't have
to cook it at all, but you
do need massive muscles.*

*I firmly believe coconut
ice should be pink, really pink.
This is not a moment to get
all modern idealist with me,
young lady. What harm can
a drop of pink really do?
Remember when you were
six years old and ate worms,
nothing bad ever happened,
did it?*

Takes 30 minutes to make;
set overnight.

500g (1lb 2oz) icing sugar
400g can condensed milk
400g (14oz) desiccated coconut
pink food colouring

⬤ Line a 20cm (8in) square baking tin (4cm/1½in deep)
with cling film.

⬤ Sift the icing sugar into a bowl, then add the condensed
milk and, starting with a wooden spoon, stir the mixture.
Then roll up your sleeves, get stuck in with your hands
and knead the mixture.

⬤ Gradually add the coconut, kneading the stiffening mixture
until all the coconut is mixed in. It's hard work and takes
a little while, but just think of someone you don't like that
much – your boss perhaps. I like to think of Mr Greenwood
and his cartoon snoring.

⬤ Split the mixture in half. Press the first half into the
lined baking tin, pressing it down with heel of your hand.
Colour the remaining half pink using the food colouring –
it can be as pink as you wish. Mix it well.

⬤ Take small balls of the pink mix and place them over
the white coconut mix in the tin. With your hand, press
the pink mixture over the white to form an even layer.

⬤ Allow to set for a few hours – overnight is best. Use
a sharpish knife to cut into squares.

COFFEE
WALNUT WHIPS

a grown-up version for licking

MAKES

II

GLOOPY WHIPS

Whatever happened to the Coffee Walnut Whip? Whatever happened to the Walnut Whip that had two walnuts? Here is a rather grown-up version of the walnut whip, made using a gooey, coffee filling. If you are like me, then you will, without shame, bite off the walnut then stick your tongue in and wiggle it about.

Take around 30 minutes to make, plus 1 hour chilling and overnight setting.

milk chocolate, for tempering
2 tbsp coffee essence
½ tbsp soft light brown sugar
50g (2oz) milk chocolate, chopped
11 walnuts

You will also need an 11-hole fluted cup chocolate mould (please see page 186 for stockists)

❀ Temper the milk chocolate (see page 11) and use a clean, grease-free brush or teaspoon to coat and line each of the fluted cups in the mould with the chocolate. You need to do this faster than a ferret up a trouser leg or the chocolate will go thick and be rendered useless. Use a spatula to scrape away any chocolate from the top of the mould. Scrape any chocolate that you haven't used into a bowl and save to use again. Put the moulds in the fridge to set for around 20 minutes.

❀ Put the coffee essence in a measuring jug and add enough cold water to make it up to 50ml (2fl oz). Pour into a pan, add the sugar and bring to the boil. Simmer for 1 minute.

❀ Put the chopped milk chocolate in a bowl and splosh the coffee liquid over. Stir well, making sure all the chocolate has melted, and leave until cold.

❀ Take the mould out of the fridge. Spoon the chocolate and coffee mixture into the fluted cups and leave to set overnight.

❀ Temper the remaining milk chocolate, or use the tempered chocolate left over from earlier (you might need to add some more chocolate), and using a teaspoon spoon it over the ganache to cover. Crown with a walnut. Chill for at least 30 minutes until set, then carefully upturn the mould onto a board to release the walnut whips.

MIXED HIGH-CLASS CHOCOLATES AND FINEST AMERICAN, SWISS AND
FRENCH SPECIALITIES. (See Chapter XI)

No. 1.—Piped Truffle Chocolates.
No. 2.—Fruit Cream Bon-bons, decorated.
No. 3.—Finest Assorted Bon-bons, decorated, and
Parisian Creams.

No. 4.—Marzipan Cream Ch
various shapes and flavours
No. 5.—Chocolates made in Blo
with finest Creams and Past
No. 6.—Fondant Cream Chocola

SQUIRREL NIBBLES

courtesy of Squirrel Greenwood's mum

MAKES

25–30
NUTTY NIBBLES

One day Squirrel Greenwood said to himself, 'I will hop, I will skip, to the Great Oak Wood where I will play with the wood sprites and gather nuts and ting.' Before long it was really dark and a bit spooky, Squirrel Greenwood was cold and tired and really missed his mummy. Luckily, he had left a trail of acorns which, by the light of Lady Moon, he was able to follow all the way back to his yard. His mother was well vexed and grounded him for a week.

Take 20 minutes to make; about 2 hours in total to cool and set.

200g (7oz) hazelnuts
100g (4oz) flaked almonds
200g (7oz) dark chocolate,
   for tempering
a small pinch of salt

⚜ Preheat the oven to 200°C/400°F/Gas 6. Line a 39 × 35cm (15¼ × 13¾in) baking sheet with baking parchment.
⚜ Spread the nuts out over another baking sheet and place in the oven for 5–10 minutes until the nuts are toasty and golden. Remove from the oven and leave to cool.
⚜ Temper the chocolate following the method on page 11.
⚜ Once the choccy has been tempered, stir in the roasted nuts.
⚜ Using a teaspoon or two, take a dollop of the nutty chocolate mixture and place it on the prepared baking sheet. Try to keep the nut piles tall rather than flat (squirrels are notoriously fussy).
⚜ Set aside to cool and set for a couple of hours. When you can no longer bear the anticipation, eat them with aplomb.

Handy Hint
You can add a handful of chopped dried figs to the chocolate for a little extra chewiness.

MR GREENWOOD'S BUTTERED BRAZILS

Mr Greenwood's secret to happiness

MAKES
20–25
BUTTERED NUTS

Mr Greenwood has long believed that the secret to happiness is a glass of Islay malt whisky, a documentary about rough seas, a roaring fire, a dish of Buttered Brazils and me snuggled up with him on the sofa. He is not far wrong.

Take 30 minutes to make;
1 hour to cool and set.

200g (7oz) Brazil nuts
225g (8oz) soft light
   brown sugar
75g (3oz) unsalted butter
½ tsp cream of tartar
50ml (2fl oz) water
groundnut oil, for greasing

❋ Preheat the oven to 180°C/350°F/Gas 4.

❋ Scatter the Brazil nuts over a baking sheet and pop them in the oven for 10 minutes until slightly roasted and golden. Set aside to cool.

❋ Place the sugar, butter, cream of tartar and water in a deep, heavy-bottomed pan and set over a low heat, stirring until the sugar has dissolved. (You can check the sugar has dissolved by running a metal spoon through the mixture and looking on the back of the spoon for sugar crystals.)

❋ Put the sugar thermometer in the pan and bring the mixture up to the boil, without stirring. Carefully let it bubble until the thermometer reaches 130°C (266°F).

❋ Lightly oil a 39 × 35cm (15¼ × 13¾in) baking sheet. Remove the pan from the heat and, using two forks, dip each Brazil nut slowly and carefully into the hot toffee, briefly returning the toffee to the heat if it starts to dry.

❋ Place the toffee-coated Brazils on a clean baking sheet. Drizzle over any toffee left in the pan. Leave for an hour to cool and set.

❋ Keep the nuts in a cool, dry cupboard and they will last for a good five days or so.

JEWELLED FLORENTINES

for a night at the opera

MAKES

24

BISCUITS

Giacomo Moretti, the great opera singer, insisted that his favourite baker deliver these cherry, pineapple, blueberry and angelica Florentines to his dressing room at the opera house in Florence.

Take 40 minutes to make, plus setting.

40g (1½oz) mixed dried fruit, such as soured cherries, pineapple, blueberries and crystallised angelica
40g (1½oz) mixed nuts, such as hazelnuts and almonds, chopped
2 tsp rice flour
50g (2oz) plain flour
1 tbsp golden syrup
50g (2oz) golden caster sugar
50g (2oz) unsalted butter
110g (4oz) white chocolate

● Preheat the oven to 180°C/350°F/Gas 4. Line a couple of 39 × 35cm (15¼ × 13¾in) baking sheets with baking parchment.
● Introduce the fruit and angelica to your favourite mixing bowl and toss in the nuts. Add the flours and jiggle everything together. I know you know how.
● Put the golden syrup, sugar and butter in a pan and heat gently to dissolve the sugar and melt the butter. Simmer for 1 minute.
● Pour this toffee mixture into the bowl of fruits and stir together. Spoon half teaspoons of the mixture onto the parchment – about 2.5cm (1in) apart – and bake for around 12 minutes until golden. Cool on the baking sheet until firm enough to lift, then use a palette knife to transfer them to a wire rack to cool completely.
● Heat 5cm (2in) water in a pan. Pop a heatproof bowl on top of the pan, making sure the bottom of the bowl is not touching the water. Place the chocolate in the bowl and melt it gently – don't stir it otherwise it may turn into a thick mess.
● Spoon a little chocolate onto the base of each Florentine and smooth to cover. Leave until almost set, then use a fork to make a wavy pattern down the middle of the chocolate. Leave to set completely.

{ **TRIVIA**
Moretti's opera career was tragically cut short after being hit by a tram while crossing the road to the baker's. Bada bing. }

CHOCOLATE & PISTACHIO PALMIERS

pass the elephant ears

MAKES

22

FRONDY BISCUITS

The word 'palmier' literally means 'palm tree', as indeed these chocolate-filled, caramelised, crispy, puff pastry treats look rather like palm fronds. Tragically, they are also known as 'elephant ears' and 'pig ears'. I almost cried a little.

Take 30 minutes to make, plus chilling.

a little plain flour for
   rolling out
½ × 500g pack puff pastry
4–5 level tbsp chocolate
   hazelnut spread
25g (1oz) unsalted shelled
   pistachios, finely chopped
golden granulated sugar,
   to sprinkle

❀ Line two 39 × 35cm (15¼ × 13¾in) baking sheets with greaseproof paper.

❀ Dust a clean work surface with flour. Roll the oblong of puff pastry to make a rectangle measuring about 28 × 18cm (11 × 7in). Roll the pastry one way only, otherwise the puff pastry won't rise evenly; now that is what I call a handy hint.

❀ Spread the pastry with the chocolate hazelnut gloop then scatter over the pistachios. Press them into the spread. Roll the longest sides of the rectangle in towards each other until they meet in the middle, pressing the pastry down firmly as you go. Press the two joins together, then turn over and pop on one of the lined baking sheets. Chill for 20–30 minutes. Preheat the oven to 220°C/425°F/Gas 7.

❀ Take the pastry roll out of the fridge and put it on a board. Slice it into 5mm–1cm (¼–½in) pieces from one end, working down to the other. Lay the pastries flat-side down on the prepared greaseproof, then lightly roll each one with the rolling pin to flatten. Sprinkle with sugar, then bake in the oven for 10–15 minutes until golden and crisp.

PEANUT BUTTER & JELLY TRUFFLES

ready? steady? dribble!

MAKES
27
'AWESOME' NUGGETS

Hot diggety dawg, a layer of salty, peanut butter ganache upon which perches a wobble of raspberry jam, the whole shameless nugget then swathed in dark chocolate. Salivate, salivate. I have tried this recipe on Squirrel Greenwood who pronounced it, 'da boom'.

Take 40 minutes to make, plus chilling and setting.

40g (1½oz) unsalted peanuts
a good pinch of sea salt
50ml (2fl oz) double cream
5g (¼oz) salted butter
25g (½oz) milk chocolate,
　very finely chopped
2 tsp raspberry conserve,
　plus extra to decorate
freeze-dried raspberry bits
300g (9oz) dark chocolate,
　for tempering

You will also need a 27-hole chocolate log mould (see page 186 for stockists)

❀ Stick the peanuts in a pan and add the salt. Now dry-fry over a medium heat until lovely and golden. Tip them into a mini food processor, then cool for about 10 minutes.

❀ Pulse the nuts until very finely ground, then whizz until the mixture comes together and makes peanut butter. Well done.

❀ Please pour the cream into a pan and add the butter. Bring the mixture gently to the boil. Turn the heat off underneath the pan and throw in the chocolate. Shake the pan a bit, swirling all the mixture together so that the chocolate melts into a yummy, even squidge.

❀ Stir in the peanut butter and spoon into a bowl. Chill for an hour to firm up.

❀ Temper the dark chocolate, following the method on page 11. Use to line the holes in the mould, then scrape off any bits around the edges. Reserve the remaining chocolate and place the mould in the fridge to set.

❀ Fill each hole with a little raspberry conserve and a pinch of freeze-dried raspberry bits. Top with a little of the peanut ganache. Chill the mould again.

❀ Temper the remaining chocolate and use to encase the ganache filling, taking care not to let it dribble onto the edges of the mould. Chill again for 10 minutes until set, then turn out on to a board and serve.

PISTACHIO KATLI

delicate golden cardamom leaves

This is my version of the stunning Indian sweet, usually made from cashews and often served at weddings. Mine are made from pistachios and cardamom and shaped into leaves. An Indian prince once gave his bride-to-be a gift of katli on their wedding day. Following a procession of 100 bejewelled donkeys, the prince, crowned with pearls and tinkling gold bells, arrived on an elephant, with a tray laden with sweets. I give it six months.

Take 40 minutes to make.

50g (2oz) shelled unsalted
   pistachios
35g (1½oz) salted butter
125ml (4½fl oz) water
50g (2oz) caster sugar
50g (2oz) ground almonds
½ tbsp whole milk
finely grated zest ½ orange
seeds from 2 cardamom
   pods, finely ground
icing sugar, for dusting
edible gold dust

You will also need a 3cm leaf-shaped cutter (see page 186 for stockists).

❀ Pulse the pistachios in a blender until finely ground. Don't whizz the machine furiously otherwise the nuts will be oily. Take your frustration out on the cat.

❀ Put the butter in a pan and melt slowly over a low heat. As soon as all the butter has melted, skim off any scum and pour the golden liquid beneath into a cup. Discard any milky solids at the bottom.

❀ Pour the water into a heavy-bottomed pan and add the sugar. Heat gently to dissolve. Bring to the boil, stirring all the time until the sugar syrup starts to form little strands when you lift the spoon – it'll take around 3–5 minutes for this to happen.

❀ Stir in the ground pistachios, ground almonds, butter, milk, orange zest and ground cardamom and stir well to mix everything together. Cook the mixture over a low heat for 2–3 minutes, beating all the time until it starts to look like a paste. It'll look very like a soft marzipan. Turn the heat off and continue to beat for a minute or two in the heat left in the pan.

❀ Tip the mixture into a bowl and cool for 5 minutes, then knead well until the mixture looks shiny.

❀ Dust a piece of baking parchment with icing sugar and put the nutty mixture on top. Cover with another piece of baking parchment. Roll the mixture a little to make it a bit flatter. Recover with the baking parchment and continue to roll until very thin – just a couple of millimetres thick will do it.

❀ Dust lightly with icing sugar then use the leaf cutter to stamp out the shapes. If the leaves stick to the cutter, use a palette knife to gently ease the point out and peel off. Dust the edges with edible glittery stuff and serve.

PEANUT BUTTERFLIES

oozy, salty, peanut butter gloop

MAKES
9
FLUTTERBIES

Now, you know I am very fond of peanut butter, I have told you a thousand times – have you forgotten already? Please try to keep up. Here is a revelation: little milk chocolate butterflies filled with oozy, salty, peanut butter gloop. Make them, eat them, take a satisfied nap in a pot of sunny geraniums.

Take about 30 minutes to make, plus 1 hour chilling.

milk chocolate, for tempering
50g (2oz) smooth peanut butter
10g (½oz) double cream
25g (1oz) soft light brown
   sugar

You will also need a 9-hole butterfly chocolate mould (please see the end of this book for stockists)

❀ Temper the chocolate (see page 11) and use an unsullied, grease-free brush or teaspoon to coat and line each of the butterfly holes in the mould with the chocolate. Do this quickly otherwise the chocolate will cool and become too thick to work with – like Mavis in accounts. Use a spatula to scrape away any chocolate from the top of the mould. Scrape any chocolate that you haven't used into a bowl and save to use again. Put the moulds in the fridge to set for around 20 minutes.

❀ Put the peanut butter, cream and sugar in a pan and heat gently, allowing the peanut butter to melt. Stir together and sing a little tune – la-la-la. Spoon the mixture into the set chocolate butterflies and level the tops of each one. Chill to allow the mixture to firm up.

❀ Take the mould out of the fridge and allow it to come up to room temperature. Temper the reserved leftover chocolate (you might need to add some more), and spoon over the peanut butter cream to cover. Chill for 30 minutes to set. Gently upturn onto a board – the butterflies should easily slide out like a bendy bus from a junction.

Sugar Gossip
Dates for your Diary
The Good News is that 24 January is National Peanut Butter Day in the USA; the Bad News is that on 2 November they celebrate National Deviled Egg Day.

SISIN

a delightful honey sesame crunch

MAKES

22

SQUARES, PLUS LOTS
OF TRIMMINGS

Whilst Sisin looks rather ordinary, it has a wealth of hidden treasures: crunchy black and white sesame seeds, stirred with a sticky caramel. If you are a panto fan you may know that the phrase 'open sesame' uttered by Aladdin as he enters the cave of treasure originates from the suprise 'pop' a sesame fruit makes when it ripens and splits.

Takes 20 minutes to make, plus setting.

vegetable oil, for brushing
75g (3oz) sesame seeds
25g (1oz) black sesame seeds
175g (6oz) caster sugar
2 tbsp clear honey

Please line a baking sheet with tin foil and brush with oil.

Be so kind as to toast the sesame seeds in a pan, tossing enthusiastically every now and then. They'll start to look a bit greasy, then they will gradually colour and look like wet sand. Remove from the heat and transfer to a bowl.

Now stick the sugar into a heavy-bottomed pan and heat gently to melt it. After about 5–10 minutes, when the sugar is starting to turn liquid at the edges, add the honey. Continue to cook the sugar over a very low heat, wiggling the pan every now and then until the mixture turns to glorious caramel – it should be the colour of an Essex spray tan. Pour onto the sesame seeds and stir well, then straightaway pour onto the oiled foil.

Spread out the mix with the back of an oiled spoon until level. Score with a knife into squares cut out the squares while still warm. Store in an airtight container for up to three days (if they last that long).

Miss Hope's Tip
If you want to dip these in chocolate, follow the tempering instructions on page 11, then hold each square by a corner and plunge.

CHAPTER
№5
CHEWY

UNICORN MALLOWPOPS

the happiest days of my life

MAKES
6
FAIRYTALE LOLLIES

I once kept a unicorn as a pet; she was called Jenny. I brushed her golden mane every day with a pure bristle hairbrush and polished her horn with beeswax until it shone. They were the happiest days of my life. One day I came home to find Mr G had sold her to the circus, where she now performs the jaw-dropping triple somersault with Tony Curtis.

Take 20 minutes to make; a couple of hours to set.

100g (4oz) sweet
   microwaveable popcorn
50g (2oz) unsalted butter
200g (7oz) pink and white
   marshmallows
groundnut oil, for greasing

You will also need
6 wooden lolly sticks

❧ Following the packet instructions, place the popcorn in the microwave and pop it. Open the bag and pour the popcorn into a large bowl. Eat a handful. (Oh, come on, don't pretend you don't want to, no one is looking and I won't tell.)

❧ Put the butter into a pan and melt it gently. Add the mallows and cook on a low heat for 10 minutes, stirring from time to time, until the mallows have melted.

❧ Pour the mallow mess over the popcorn and stir it around and around, like a record, baby. Leave the mallow and popcorn muddle to cool for about 30 minutes.

❧ Take a lump of the mixture, a little larger than a golf ball, and squeeze the mixture into a cone or horn shape between your hands. Really give it a good squeeze so that all the popcorn sticks together firmly. This is enjoyably squidgy and sticky – well, I enjoy it anyway. Place on a lightly oiled 39 × 35cm (15¼ × 13¾in) baking sheet to set.

❧ Leave to set for a couple of hours, then push a lolly stick into the wide base of each cone and munch away.

ROSE & PISTACHIO TURKISH DELIGHT

soft and bouncy

MAKES

30

ROSY JELLIES

Sugar Trivia

Turkish delight can be found in Charles Dickens's **The Mystery of Edwin Drood** as 'lumps of delight'; it is also the confection to which Edmund succumbs in **The Lion, The Witch and The Wardrobe**, and it features in Madonna's song 'Candy Shop'.

Turkish delight was originally eaten as a cure for sore throats. Known as 'lokum rahat', it literally translates as 'throat's ease'. This sweetly scented rose and pistachio Turkish delight is soft and bouncy. It takes an age to make, but it is really worth the effort.

Takes 1½ hours to make; chill and set overnight.

groundnut oil, for greasing
900g (2lb) granulated sugar
1 tbsp lemon juice
175g (6oz) cornflour
1 tsp cream of tartar
2 tbsp rose syrup
2–3 drops pink food colouring
100g (4oz) shelled
   unsalted pistachios
icing sugar, to dust
cornflour, to dust

Line a 20cm (8in) square baking tin (4cm/1½in deep) with baking parchment and lightly oil it with groundnut oil.

Place the sugar, lemon juice and 340ml (12fl oz) water in a pan and put it over a low heat. Stir until all the sugar has dissolved. Bring the mixture to the boil, without stirring, and slowly, using your sugar thermometer, bring the mixture up to 118°C (245°F) – this will take about 15 minutes.

Meanwhile, in a separate pan (this one must be really deep and truly heavy bottomed), place 570ml (1 pint) cold water, the cornflour and the cream of tartar. Give it a good stir and place over a low heat. Keep stirring so that there are no lumps (it's like making cheese sauce). Bring to the boil and beat quickly until the mixture looks like wallpaper paste. Take it off the heat.

Place the cornflour mixture back on the heat as soon as the sugar mixture has reached 118°C (245°F) and pour the sugar over the cornflour mixture. Stir it well – it will look like an ocean of icebergs – and if any lumps persist, whisk them out with a metal whisk. Keeping the heat low (use a heat diffuser if you have one), bring the mixture to a geyser-plopping simmer. Let it simmer like this, plopping and sighing, for an hour – yes, an hour.

Take the pan off the heat, stir in the rose syrup, the pink food colouring (as much or as little as you like) and the pistachios. Pour the pink blubber into the prepared tin and leave to cool and set overnight. It smells amazing.

Once set, cut the Turkish delight into squares and dust with equal amounts of icing sugar and cornflour sifted together.

LEMON & BLUEBERRY NOUGAT

a white, torrone-style nougat

MAKES
25
SILKEN PIECES

There is little in this life nicer than my nougat – laden with blueberries and crystallised lemon peel. This is a white, 'torrone'-style nougat, chewy rather than hard, with a crisp rice-paper base.

Takes 40 minutes to make; cool and set overnight.

400g (14oz) granulated sugar
100ml (3½fl oz) clear honey
50ml (2fl oz) liquid glucose
2 large egg whites, at room
   temperature
a pinch of salt
50g (2oz) candied lemon
   peel, chopped
75g (3oz) flaked almonds,
   toasted
75g (3oz) dried blueberries
40g (1½oz) white chocolate
   chips
a handful of fresh blueberries

You will also need a sheet
of rice paper

❧ Line a 17cm (6¾in) square tin with baking parchment, allowing the paper to come up the sides. Cut a square of rice paper the same size as the base and put on top of the parchment.

❧ Put the sugar, honey and liquid glucose in a large heavy-bottomed pan (I use a deep 24cm (9½in) diameter pan) with 125ml (4½fl oz) cold water. Heat gently to dissolve the sugar. Pop a sugar thermometer in the pan and bring the mixture to the boil. Allow it to bubble until the temperature reaches 125°C (257°F). At this point, put the egg whites in the bowl of a freestanding mixer and slowly whisk until stiff peaks form, taking care not to overbeat. Fill your sink with 10cm cold water.

❧ Continue to cook the syrup until the thermometer reaches 149°C (300°F) – it should be a dark caramel colour. Dip the base of the pan in the water to stop the caramel cooking.

❧ Slowly pour the caramel into the food mixer; it will froth up to the top of the mixing bowl. Add the salt. Mix on a moderate speed for 5–8 minutes to incorporate all the syrup. Now you can turn the mixer off.

❧ Fold in the candied peel, most of the almonds and the dried blueberries then spoon into the tin, smoothing it down with a wet knife. Sprinkle over the white chocolate chips with the remaining almonds and the blueberries and leave to cool. Leave to set overnight before cutting into squares.

CHERRY & ALMOND NOUGAT

my best friend

MAKES

20

STICKY LUMPS

Sticky but firm, oozy and sweet, I'd like to make this nougat my best friend; we could cuddle up at the pictures together and maybe stop for a shandy in the town. Why ask for the moon Cherry and Almond Nougat, when we have the stars?

Takes 30 minutes to make; cool and set overnight.

200g (7oz) whole almonds
2 large egg whites
400g (14oz) caster sugar
100ml (4fl oz) clear honey
210ml (7½fl oz) liquid glucose
200g (7oz) glacé cherries
seeds scraped from
   1 vanilla pod

You will also need 3 sheets of rice paper

◉ Preheat the oven to 200°C/400°F/Gas 6. Line a 20cm (8in) square baking tin (4cm/1½in deep) with the rice paper.
◉ Place the almonds onto a baking sheet and pop in the oven to roast for 5–10 minutes. Set aside to cool.
◉ Place the egg whites in a food mixer and whisk until stiff.
◉ Place the sugar, honey and glucose into a deep, heavy-bottomed pan. Add 2 tablespoons of water. Heat gently to dissolve the sugar. Put a sugar thermometer in the pan, bring the honey mixture to the boil and bubble until your thermometer reaches 125°C (260°F). With the food mixer running, take the pan off the heat and slowly pour half the honey mixture into the egg whites in a thin ribbon. Leave the mixer running.
◉ Quickly return the pan to the heat, increase the heat slightly, and bring the remaining honey mixture up to 157°C (315°F). The mixture should be a dark caramel colour. Pour this honey mixture into the food mixer, slowly. It will froth up to the top of the mixing bowl. Mix on a moderate speed for a full 10 minutes. Now you can turn the mixer off.
◉ Fold in the almonds, cherries and vanilla seeds; the nougat will be reasonably stiff now. Pour the nougat into the prepared tin and leave to set, preferably overnight. Cut into small squares to serve.

SALTED CARAMEL MALLOW TEACAKES

made by angels

MAKES
10–12
TEA CAKES, PLUS EXTRA
OFFCUTS TO NIBBLE ON

A divine, cloudy marshmallow made by angels, slumbering on a sticky, salted caramel with a delightful mini digestive biscuit for a mattress made from the horns of unicorns, dusted with diamonds of sea salt from the crown of Venus. Etc. etc. and so on and so forth.

Take around 45 minutes to make; about 20 minutes to bake, plus chilling.

For the mallow
a little vegetable oil
icing sugar, to dust
2 gelatine leaves (5g)
225g (8oz) granulated sugar
½ tbsp liquid glucose
1 large egg white
grated zest of 1 orange

For the biscuit base
50g (2oz) softened unsalted
    butter, plus extra to grease
50g (2oz) golden caster sugar
50g (2oz) wholemeal flour
50g (2oz) plain flour
a large pinch of salt
1 tbsp ground almonds
2 tbsp milk

❀ Make the mallow first. Oil and line a 17cm (6¾in) square tin with baking parchment, then dust lightly with icing sugar. Put the gelatine leaves in a bowl of cold water and leave to soften.

❀ Next, put the sugar, liquid glucose and 100ml (3½fl oz) cold water into a heavy-bottomed pan. Place over a low heat to dissolve the sugar, stirring from time to time. Put a sugar thermometer into the pan and increase the heat slightly. Watch the temperature carefully. When it reaches around 120°C (248°F), start to whisk the egg white and whisk until stiff. A freestanding mixer is best for this, or use a bowl and an electric hand whisk.

❀ As soon as the syrup reaches 127°C (260°F), drain the gelatine leaves, then take the pan off the heat and, using a large metal spoon, stir in the gelatine and orange zest. Gradually start to pour the syrup into the bowl, whisking all the time. As soon as all the syrup is added, continue to whisk on high speed for about 8 minutes until thickened and the mixture has cooled.

❀ Spoon into the prepared tin, spreading it out into the corners. You may find it easier to do this with a wet knife. Leave to set.

❀ Make the biscuits. Beat the butter and sugar together in a bowl. Once the mixture has come together and looks creamy, sift in the two types of flour. Work them into the mixture with

To pimp the teacakes
fudge sauce and/
    or raspberry jam
75g (3oz) dark chocolate
sea salt flakes

the salt and ground almonds until it looks crumbly, then drizzle over the milk and bring it together with your hands. Wrap in baking parchment and chill for 20 minutes.

🍪 Preheat the oven to 180°C/350°F/Gas 4. Roll out the biscuit dough on a board until 3mm ($1/8$ in) thick. Stamp out rounds using a 5cm cutter and chill again on a greased baking sheet. Chill for 15 minutes.

🍪 Bake for 20–25 minutes until golden. Cool on a wire rack.

🍪 Put a tray or baking sheet under the wire rack. Spread each biscuit with fudge sauce or jam, leaving a little border round the edge. Stamp out rounds of marshmallow using a 4cm cutter and pop the mallows on top of the biscuits.

🍪 Melt the chocolate in a heatproof bowl set over a pan of simmering water, making sure the base of the bowl doesn't touch the water. Drizzle all over the biscuits.

🍪 Melt a couple of tablespoons of fudge sauce in a pan (or in the microwave) and drizzle over the top to finish. Sprinkle with sea salt if you fancy. Sticky boomba.

SWEET SUSHI

more like a craft class than a baking day

MAKES
20
SUSHIS

We've had such a lot of fun in the Sugar HQ kitchen playing with this crazy recipe. It's more like a craft class than a baking day. Crispies bound with melted marshmallows and golden syrup make up the 'rice' base whilst I used my Apricot Leather Belts (see page 179) for the seaweed and candy shrimps; fondant fish sit on top.

My dear Japanese chum Tito has this message for you, "このお菓子は食べちゃダメよ、*Miss Hope* はちょっと変わってるから"

Takes around 20 minutes to make the sushi rice and about 1 hour to decorate.

For the 'sticky rice'
100g (4oz) pink marshmallows
40g (1½oz) unsalted butter
1 tbsp golden syrup
100g (4oz) puffed rice
a good pinch of sea salt
icing sugar, for dusting

🍃 Put the marshmallows, butter and golden syrup into a pan and heat gently. Allow the marshmallows to melt, stirring well from time to time.

🍃 Take the pan off the heat and stir in the puffed rice. Wet your hands well – I love this part – then take a large teaspoon of the mixture and shape it into an oval, flattening it down. Tap it lightly to flatten off the base and place on a board lined with baking parchment. Shape about two thirds of the mixture in this way (this should make 15 ovals). Then shape the rest of the mixture into little bite-size cylinders (about 5). Rub each base with a little icing sugar and place on baking parchment to dry before decorating.

🍃 Roll out five small pieces of green fondant and wrap around the cylinders (they should be tall enough so that they stand up a little taller than the cylinders) to make sweet 'nori' (seaweed). Roll small bits of orange into rounds to make 'salmon eggs'. Pop inside the green roll, on top of the puffed rice cylinder and brush with orange food paste.

🍃 For mackerel sushi, take a small piece of white fondant and shape it into a rectangular fish fillet shape, tapering it thinly at one end (this is the bit by the tail) and thicker at the top (the bit by the head). Paint a thin line of purple food paste along one edge of each. Wipe the brush and dip it into the

➤

To pimp the sticky rice
green fondant
orange fondant
white fondant
orange food colouring paste
purple food colouring paste
blue food colouring paste
Apricot Leather Belts
    (see page 179)
shrimp sweets
a little icing sugar,
    for rolling out

blue and flick down along the purple edge to create
the shimmering silver effect of mackerel skin.

❀ For prawn sushi, cut small fish shapes, about the size
of the top of the oval-shapes made from the marshmallow
and puffed rice mixture, out of a little piece of rolled-out
white fondant. Roll them out again to flatten slightly. Put
on top of the rice ovals, then draw a line down the middle
using a small sharp knife. Paint orange food paste flicking
it outwards from this line to the edge so it looks like
a cooked prawn.

❀ For shrimp sushi, use a sharp knife or pizza roller
to cut thin strips of the apricot leather belts. Rest a
shrimp sweet on top of the rice ovals, then wrap a strip
of the leather around it, sealing it underneath. Job done.

SALTY DOGS

*truly over-the-top
toffee squidginess*

MAKES

8

GOOEY BARS

*This truly over-the-top, milk
chocolate nutty bar hides a
bucketful of marshmallows,
a truck load of puffed rice and
a vat of peanuts embedded
in 10 tons of caramel with
a sprinkle of sea salt.*

Take around 30 minutes
to make.

25g (1oz) salted butter
75g (3oz) milk chocolate,
   broken into squares
110g (4½oz) marshmallows
2 tbsp chocolate malt powder
40g (1½oz) puffed rice cereal
200g (7oz) toffees
2 tbsp milk
a large pinch of sea salt
50g (2oz) salted roasted
   peanuts

● First up, put the butter, chocolate and marshmallows
in a heavy-based pan and heat gently, cooking until all the
ingredients have melted. Stir every now and then with
a wooden spoon to mix them together. Don't overstir it.
Top stuff.

● Scrape the mixture into a bowl and give it a good thrashing
to cool it down quickly and thicken it. Stir in the malt powder,
then fold in the puffed rice. Tip out of the bowl and onto
a board.

● Shape into a rough rectangle and cut 8 bars along the
width. Shape each one into a stubby sausage dog shape
and allow to cool on a board.

● Put the toffees and milk into a pan and allow to melt over
a low heat. Stir well to mix the two together, then stir in the salt.
Take the pan off the heat and allow to cool for a few minutes.

● Put a cooling rack on top of a board and put the caramel bars
on top. Spoon over the toffee mixture then push the salted
roasted peanuts over the top. Lick the bowl and the board.
Chill to set.

BLUEBERRY
ANISEED DIAMONDS

take your taste buds out for a jog

MAKES

50–60
EXTREMELY MOREISH
BLACK DIAMONDS

Aniseed is indeed a love/hate delicacy. As you know, I'd like to take your taste buds out for a jog so I've combined buds of star anise with blueberry syrup to make this velvety diamond 'liquorice'. Personally I love liquorice, especially the double salted variety.

Takes 45 minutes to make, plus over night chilling

a little vegetable oil,
   for greasing
50g (2oz) unsalted butter
100g (4oz) caster sugar
75g (3oz) golden syrup
75g (3oz) condensed milk
40g (1½oz) treacle
a big pinch of sea salt
75g (3oz) plain flour
2 tbsp blueberry syrup
1 tsp black food colouring paste
4 star anise pods, finely ground
   in a pestle and mortar

Grease and line a 33 × 23cm (13 × 9in) Swiss roll tin with baking parchment, then brush the parchment with a little oil.

Put the butter, sugar, golden syrup, condensed milk, treacle and salt in a pan over a medium heat and cook gently to melt the butter and dissolve the sugar.

Rest a sugar thermometer on the side of the pan and turn up the heat to medium. Bring to the boil and cook until the mixture reaches 124°C (255°F).

Take the pan off the heat and stir in the flour, blueberry syrup, food colouring and ground star anise.

Spoon into the prepared tin and cool. Transfer to the fridge and chill overnight.

Oil a large sharp knife and cut across the rectangle into 1.5cm (½in) strips. Cut down each strip to make diamonds. Use a screwdriver or other round pokey thing to mark a hole through each middle to decorate.

176
CHEWY

APRICOT LEATHER BELTS

perfect for lunch boxes

MAKES
10–12
BELTS/RESTRAINTS

My scrumptious Apricot Leather Belts are a cinch to make and a joy to chew. It is full of fresh squishy fruit pulp and totes yummy. It is also most useful for holding your trousers up and keeping your wig on in a high wind.

Takes 30 minutes to make, plus 10–12 hours to cook.

6 fresh apricots, halved, stoned and finely chopped
50g (2oz) golden caster sugar
1 lemon

⦿ Line a 33 × 23cm (13 × 9in) Swiss roll tin with microwave-safe cling film. Preheat the oven to 50°C/120°F/Gas ¼.

⦿ Place the chopped apricots in a pan with 200ml cold water, cover with a lid and place over a medium heat. Bring to a simmer and, without lifting the lid (please do try not to, you are so naughty), continue to cook for 15 minutes until the fruit is very soft.

⦿ Remove from the heat, take the lid off the pan and mash well with a potato masher. Stir in the sugar and add a good squeeze of lemon juice.

⦿ Now pop the pan back on the heat and continue to cook, uncovered, on a low to medium heat, stirring all the time for another good 10 minutes until the mixture has thickened. It's a good time to do your pelvic floor exercises.

⦿ Use a stick blender thingy to purée the fruit to ensure there are no lumps or bumps in it so the mixture is totes smooth.

⦿ Spoon into the prepared tray and level the surface. Bake in the oven for at least 10–12 hours.

⦿ By this time the paste will have dried out completely and become leathery – like Mr Greenwood. Allow to cool and carefully lift away from the cling film. Run a pizza cutter down the length of the leather to cut into strips then roll up tightly.

POPCORN ESPRESSO MACCHIATO BALLS

a rather unusual after-dinner treat

MAKES

18

BALLS

Stonkingly moreish, my popcorn balls are squidged together with marshmallow and blessed with a liberal sprinkling of crunchy, ground espresso coffee. They would make a rather unusual after-dinner treat to munch on while your guests play Snakes and Ladders.

Take around 20 minutes to make.

100g (4oz) mini marshmallows
40g (1½oz) unsalted butter
1 tbsp vegetable oil
50g (2oz) popcorn kernels
25g (½oz) white chocolate, grated
¾ tsp ground coffee

⬤ Shove the marshmallows in a pan with the butter and heat gently to melt the two together. Give it a stir every now and then to help it on its way. Turn off the heat.

⬤ Heat the oil gently in a heavy-bottomed pan and add the popcorn. Cover with a lid and allow to cook. After about 5 minutes you'll hear the corn start to pop. Toss the pan a bit, don't lift the lid you ninny. Once the corn has finished popping take it off the heat.

⬤ Pour the marshmallow mixture into the popcorn pan with the white chocolate. Sprinkle over the ground coffee and stir everything together. Cool for 5 minutes.

⬤ Don rubber gloves and take a large tablespoon of the mixture. You may want to wet the gloves at this point too. Roll and squeeze the popcorn into a ball and let it have a nap on a baking sheet. Store in an airtight container if you must.

ICE CREAM OYSTERS

pearls in a wafer shell

MAKES

6

WITH A SLICE OF NOUGAT
TO NIBBLE

Mary Higgins, the famous cross-Channel swimmer, often partook of this joyous ice cream, studded with nougat, nestling in a wafer oyster shell. After an attempt to swim the Atlantic, with only a pack of lard for company, Mary was washed up on a desert island where she lived happily for years playing with starfish.

Take 1½ hours to make, plus freezing.

For the nougat
200g (7oz) granulated sugar
50ml (2fl oz) clear honey
25ml (1fl oz) liquid glucose
1 large egg white
100g (4 oz) chopped mixed
    dried fruit, such as
    pineapple, glacé cherry
    and ginger
1 tsp vanilla extract
rice paper

For the ice cream
75g (3oz) granulated sugar
3 large egg yolks
seeds scraped from
    ½ vanilla pod
600ml carton double cream
6 oyster wafer shells

- Line a 15 × 18cm (6 × 7in) shallow baking tin with rice paper.
- Make the ice cream. Put the sugar and 150ml (5fl oz) water into a small pan. Heat gently to dissolve the sugar then bring to the boil and boil for 3 minutes. Set aside to cool for 3 minutes.
- Whisk the egg yolks in a bowl, then pour the sugar syrup over the yolks, taking care not to let the syrup fall on to the whisk. Keep whisking until the mixture doubles and triples in volume and rises up the bowl in a big frothy mass. Fold in the vanilla seeds and cream then spoon into a container. Freeze for 2 hours.
- For the nougat, put the sugar, honey, glucose and 2 tablespoons of cold water into a small heavy-bottomed pan. Heat gently. As soon as the sugar has dissolved put a sugar thermometer into the pan and increase the heat slightly.
- Cook until the temperature reaches 120°C (250°F). At this point, whisk the egg white until stiff peaks form. Fill the sink with cold water. Watch the temperature carefully and as soon as it reaches 149°C (300°F), dip the base of the pan into the sink to cool the syrup. With the motor running, pour the syrup steadily over the egg whites and whisk in for 5–10 minutes. Fold in the dried fruit. Spoon into the tin, flattening down with a wet knife and cover with another piece of rice paper. Leave to set.
- Whisk the ice cream again, then freeze for another 2 hours.
- Cut the nougat in half then break off little chunks from half and fold it into the almost-set ice cream. Keep the other half wrapped in baking parchment to nibble on. Freeze the ice cream for 2 hours. To serve, dip a scoop into boiling water and shape the ice cream into balls. Spoon two or three into each wafer shell.

CANDIED PEEL & WHITE CHOCOLATE NOUGAT

probably the best nougat in the world

MAKES
25–30
SQUARES

If you are short of time and don't want to make your own candied peel (even though it is the best candied peel in the world and can be found on pages 93–95) you will find suppliers of good candied peel on page 186.

Takes 30 minutes
to make; cool and
set overnight.

100g (4oz) white chocolate, broken into little bits
2 large egg whites
400g (14oz) caster sugar
125ml (4½fl oz) clear honey
210ml (7½fl oz) liquid glucose
a pinch of salt
seeds scraped from 1 vanilla pod
200g (7oz) candied peel (lemon, orange or grapefruit), roughly chopped

You will also need
3 sheets of rice paper

● Line a 20cm (8in) square baking tin (4cm/1½in deep) with the rice paper.

● If you are making your own candied peel, do this first – simply follow my recipe on pages 93–95 but do not add the chocolate coating.

● Put the chocolate bits into a freezer bag and put it in the freezer, where it will play hospitals with the fish fingers.

● Place the egg whites in a food mixer and whisk until stiff.

● Place the sugar, honey and liquid glucose into a deep heavy-bottomed pan and add 2 tablespoons of water. Heat gently until the sugar has dissolved.

● Place a sugar thermometer in the pan, bring the honey mixture to the boil and bubble until the temperature reaches 125°C (260°F), the mixture should be a buttery, golden colour. This takes 10–15 minutes. With the food mixer running, take the pan off the heat and pour half the honey mixture into the egg white in a thin ribbon, slowly does it. Leave the mixer running until I tell you to stop.

● Quickly return the pan to the heat, increase the heat slightly and bring the honey mixture up to 157°C (315°F) on your sugar thermometer. This will take 10 minutes. The mixture should be a dark, caramel colour. Pour the remaining honey mixture into the food mixer, slowly. Add the salt and the vanilla seeds then mix on a moderate speed for a full 10 minutes.

● Now you can turn the mixer off.

● Next, take the chocolate out of the freezer and fold it and the candied peel into the nougat – it will be fairly stiff.

● Pour the nougat into the prepared tin and leave it to set, preferably overnight. Cut into small squares when firm.

SUGAR FACT

Nougat is called torrone *in Italy and* turrón *in Spain. You say potayto, I say patarto.*

Handy Hint
If this recipe does not set it is because you have:
a) Ignored the temperatures like a crazy person, or,
b) Not beaten it for long enough.

STOCKISTS

Here is a list of jolly stockists where you'll find some of the more troublesome ingredients and items used in my recipes. As if by magic (a click of a button or a tinkle on the phone), wonderful goodies will be delivered to your kitchen.

BAKING SHEETS AND TINS, BISCUIT CUTTERS, SUGAR THERMOMETERS, HEAT-RESISTANT MATS, BAKING SCRAPERS, LOLLY STICKS, TOFFEE TRAYS AND TOFFEE HAMMERS.
www.lakeland.co.uk
www.squires-shop.com
www.hobbycraft.co.uk

EDIBLE GOLD LEAF, CRYSTALLISED ROSE AND VIOLET PETALS (OH, THE BEAUTY), REAL FRUIT FONDANT ICING, SILVER BALLS, LEAF-SHAPED CUTTERS, SWEET AND PETIT FOUR CASES.
www.jane-asher.co.uk
www.squires-shop.com

HEART-SHAPED CUTTERS AND FLOWER CUTTERS.
www.cakecraftshop.co.uk

ROSE AND VIOLET SYRUPS AND CANDIED PEEL.
www.melburyandappleton.co.uk

ROSEHIP SYRUP.
www.lakeland.co.uk

EDIBLE LUSTRE DUSTS.
www.cakescookiesandcraftsshop.co.uk

INDEX

THANK YOUS

MISS HOPE AND MR GREENWOOD

Ginormous hugs and unreserved adoration to our sweet family: Cristian Barnett, Imogen Fortes and Emma Marsden. Perfect from every angle.

SCREENCHANNEL

Thanks to Emma Willis and Maxine Watson at the BBC. Thanks to the amazing production team who managed to control themselves sufficiently to film the sweets before eating them, and of course thanks to Miss H and Mr G for their indefatigable good humour, wit and skill in this first foray onto our screens.

This book is published to accompany the television series entitled
Sweets Made Simple, first broadcast on BBC Two in 2014.

screenchannel
television

BBC commissioning executives: Emma Willis and Maxine Watson
Executive Producers: Emma Barker and Peter Lowe
Series Director: Ed St Giles
Series Producer: Melanie Jappy
Series Home Economists: Emma Marsden and David Birt

10 9 8 7 6 5 4 3 2 1

Published in 2014 by BBC Books, an imprint of Ebury Publishing.
A Penguin Random House Group Company.

Text copyright pages 25, 78, 114, 120, 136, 179–180 © Screenchannel Television Limited 2014
All other text copyright © Miss Hope 2009, 2011
Screenchannel logo © Screenchannel Television Limited

Photography by Cristian Barnett; pages 27, 32, 44, 47, 77, 82, 86,
90, 100, 108, 119, 129, 128, 143, 144, 163 and 166 by Dan Jones
Design by Smith and Gilmour

Miss Hope and Screenchannel Television have asserted their
right to be identified as the authors of this Work in accordance
with the Copyright, Designs and Patents Act 1988.

All rights reserved. No part of this publication may be reproduced,
stored in a retrieval system, or transmitted in any form or by any
means, electronic, mechanical, photocopying, recording or otherwise,
without the prior permission of the copyright owner.

The Random House Group Limited Reg. No. 954009

Addresses for companies within the Random House Group
can be found at www.randomhouse.co.uk

A CIP catalogue record for this book is available from the British Library.

ISBN: 978 1 849 90823 8

The Random House Group Limited supports The Forest Stewardship Council
(FSC®), the leading international forest certification organisation. Our books
carrying the FSC label are printed on FSC® certified paper. FSC is the only forest
certification scheme endorsed by the leading environmental organisations,
including Greenpeace. Our paper procurement policy can be found at
www.randomhouse.co.uk/environment

FSC
www.fsc.org
MIX
Paper from
responsible sources
FSC® C004592

Colour origination by AltaImage, London
Printed and bound in Germany by Firmengruppe APPL, aprinta druck, Wemding

To buy books by your favourite authors and register for offers visit
www.randomhouse.co.uk